IPL-2023

Mount Everest
of
Crime and Corruption

Atul Kumar

DIAMOND BOOKS

www.diamondbook.in

Publisher	:	**Diamond Pocket Books (P) Ltd.** X-30, Okhla Industrial Area, Phase-II New Delhi-110020
Phone	:	011-40712200
E-mail	:	sales@dpb.in
Website	:	www.dpb.in
Edition	:	2023
Printed by	:	Repro (India)

IPL-2023 : Mount Everest of Crime and Corruption

Author : *Atul Kumar*

Contents

Preface..5

An Overview of IPL-2023 13

1. Opening Eyes to IPL-2023...31

2. It's elementary, My dear Watson! 42

3. IPL, Betting, and Fixing...52

4. A Crime Most Extraordinary...63

5. When All Law-Enforcers became Non-Existent.................................66

6. Judiciary in the Dock 70

7. The Criminal Media...74

8. PM Modi, Politics, and Mount Everest of Corruption.........................84

9. The Mob mentality Rules..89

10. Manifestation of the Infinite Human Stupidity 99

11. Revisiting Covid Times...111

12. Myself and the World...113

About the Author...130

Preface

The Indian Premier League, popularly known as IPL, has been a Cricket Tournament taking place every year since 2008. Mostly it is held in India, but at times it has taken place abroad also. It took place alright even during Covid years. Due to its vast popularity, the tournament has now become like an annual festive season in India. But is it just a source of entertainment for the masses, a platform to groom future cricketers in India, a means to generate more revenue for BCCI for overall promotion of Cricket, a way to enrich the cricketers etc., as is popularly believed? Or is there much more to it? By the time one finishes reading this book, I am sure, one will feel stunned to know the reality. The readers will find that terming IPL-2023 as the Mount Everest of crime and corruption is an understatement rather than an overstatement.

In today's world, frauds and scams abound. These frequently make newspaper headlines. But the biggest known fraud, publicly known for more than a decade now, is hardly ever reported. Even if reported once in a blue moon, it gets very quickly brushed under the carpet. On the contrary, on a regular and daily basis, it makes headlines as something to be cherished for. The pages of daily newspapers and periodicals are full with columns singing paeans of the fraud itself and its perpetrators.

That present day Cricket is nothing but a staged drama through ball-by-ball institutional (internal) scripting is a foregone conclusion, today lying established even legally, and in full

knowledge of the Supreme Court of India. Probably more than enough has been said about it in my many previous books and the facebook page https://www.facebook.com/BettorsBeware, the last book being **'Beat the Cricket Mafia and Win (Yes, you can do it!)'**. The website **thecricketmafia.com** can be referred for more details. In addition, there have been many reports quoting me from time to time in one of the most reputed English dailies, and my published interviews in leading newspapers/ magazines. Some of those (the earlier ones) have also been chronicled in some of my books. **I am able to deliver this book on the strength of my earlier writings, or more precisely as a result of my existence so far.** The following list of my previous books on the subject with time of their publication is quite relevant to this book:

1. Inside the Boundary Line 2012 (towards end) (translated in Hindi also)

2. Bettors Beware 2013 (towards end again); Republished under the title 'All Cricket Matches are Fixed' in 2016. Only last year, by-chance I came to know that the republished title was lying listed by Mr Matt Harris among the best books on Cricket betting, with the following brief by him (https://www.itsonlycricket.com/best-books-on-cricket-betting?fbclid=IwAR1rUPNT0ZvS0Z-boNohxjK9WQhJ21fopouSx-NoFfm8nPUhSx-3wILVpSk may be referred):
   'All Cricket Matches are Fixed

   This is a pretty bold statement and one that the author, Atul Kumar, looks to back up with analysis and facts. He does this with great dedication and detail and many would find it difficult to argue with what are convincing findings throughout the book.

Of course, the suggestion that all cricket matches are fixed is not one that is widely shared around the sporting world. The conclusion that this book makes is that people should avoid cricket betting. Again, not many bettors would back up that view but it's worth reading this book for it's bold claims.'

3. Cricket the Massive Fraud December 2014 (translated in Hindi and some regional languages also)
4. Under World Cup (Media, Modis, Mudgals, Mamatas All Dial Dawood) 2016
5. We the Oodles 2020
6. What is killing us... Covid or Stupidity? 2021 (also in Hindi)
7. Beat the Cricket Mafia and Win (Yes, You can do it!) 2022 (also in Hindi)

The titles of the books at number 5 and 6 may make one wonder, but these books also deal with the dark side of Cricket. The book at serial 5 is a very important book that nails the all-powerful Supreme Court of India and Mr Vinod Rai, the then Head of the Committee of Administrators (COA), BCCI (Board of Control for Cricket in India), and hence the BCCI, with enough documentary evidence. The book at serial 6 above also deals with the subject partly. Though the title suggests otherwise, the book at serial 7 also advises the bettors to stay away from betting. It then goes on to arm those who can't stay away, so that they can protect themselves from the cricket mafia.

It saddens me and pains me that the people and the world at large still continue to be ignorant, while the perpetrators of the fraud continue to feign ignorance and act innocent, continuing

to indulge in crime and corruption that is unimaginably monumental. Much worse, **the punters around the globe still continue to lose billions of dollars daily to an all-powerful mafia**, despite my continuous efforts for more than ten long years now. The continuous elephantine crime of staging fake cricket matches takes place mainly for that money. I do hope this book will further help all, the punters and the other cricket fans, in a big way to be aware of the reality and hence gain a lot.

There is no dearth of people, more so the intellectuals, who would very naturally exclaim, "Ball-by-ball scripting? Oh! That is impossible!" **Because they still remain ignorant of the well-established fact that the opposite was impossible.** It is just impossible that the cricket matches, including in IPL, are not scripted ball-by-all. And it is no rocket science to see that. Continuous application of common-sense to the cricket one views in IPL matches or in other international or league matches, alone should make things clear to any open mind. Care has to be taken that one doesn't let one's own common-sense get influenced in the least by what is being told round the clock by the cricket commentators, the cricket experts, and the reputed journalists. We shall see that in more details in this book as to how and why it is so, hopefully ever most clearly.

Very few know that ball-by-ball scripting of the cricket matches including IPL matches lies mathematically and hence scientifically established for a full decade – ten long years now. Scientific proof for anything doesn't leave any doubt for any ifs and buts. **But still, to believe that all cricket matches on show including IPL matches were fixed ball-by-ball or almost so, cannot be easy for anybody**. It was not easy for me more than a decade and a half ago, when I first understood what was what, but I could understand and clearly see that it had to be so, whether I could believe it or not!

To believe that all or almost all the cricketers of past and present, all those connected with the administration of cricket or IPL, all the team owners of various teams in number of IPL type leagues being played in various countries of the world including some first world countries, all the law-enforcing agencies in India and/or abroad, the political leadership of various countries including of India, and last but not the least – the media around the world reporting on and marketing the IPL and other cricket matches as a competitive sport – all are either crooks or ignorant men and women or just self-servers, is far from easy. Impossible or almost impossible! The reality is so black and extraordinary that our normal minds fail to comprehend and/or accept it.

But ball-by-ball scripting of cricket matches we see and bet upon is an indisputable **hard fact,** reinforced many times in last ten years through a variety of sources and exposures; the latest significant one being the exposure by the arrested bookie Sanjeev Chawla. The global Media never brought even that sensational exposure much to public light. On the contrary, the media very swiftly brushed that deafening exposure under the carpet, before the masses could know about it. The culpability of a multitude of celebrities, authorities, and the all-powerful leaders – political or of the corporate world - as brought out in above para, also is undeniable; not only for ball-by-ball scripting of the cricket matches, but also for continuation of the massive fraud despite repeated public exposures for 10 long years and despite it being in full knowledge of the ICC (International Cricket Council), in full knowledge of all the authorities in cricket and outside, and of the global media for about those many years.

The fact is now also on official records, after filing of PIL through WP (C) number 1163/2017 in November 2017, in the Supreme Court of India. No authority can deny it now since

none could and did when they had the chance. They all simply have been keeping quiet, and silently but surely have been continuing with their ever-increasing criminal indulgence! Since there is no one there, no activist or leader, no celebrity, none in such a vast media, to ask them any question. There is no one from the large civil society or from the millions of intellectuals to cause them any discomfort!! The developments in the Supreme Court of India subsequent to the filing of the PIL are no less important. They all are a matter of record and well chronicled in the book 'We the Oodles.'

We just can't wish away the facts, thoroughly documented by now, by keeping our eyes closed and tightly shut and wrapping a thick black cloth around them!! Everything is so thoroughly and so indisputably documented and established, that even the all-powerful mafia consisting of and/or controlling the mighty authorities and the mightier corporate leaders has no defence whatsoever today. But alas! the tendency of a common man, including all the intellectuals, remains to believe in or go by whatever is told in the Media. Masses don't know and won't know anything that the Media deliberately hides. I don't know how many realize that Media is like an inescapable noose round the neck of the present-day society!

I am on the last leg of my journey in this world, somewhat incapacitated in the aftermath of Covid-19. So, what do I do under the circumstances? After my untiring all-out efforts for 10 long years, I make another attempt through this book to wake up the ignorantly sleeping world, awaiting ever more annihilation in the hands of the rogue forces that are in control of the political leaders and the global media. To make the world aware of and understand the prospering massive fraud and the multitude of very vast and serious implications of what

is going on. I try to do it by explaining a small sub-set of the colossal continuing international fraud and crime – IPL-2023, somewhat fresh in the memory of the readers, so that they are able to comprehend the reality of cricket and hence of all that has been happening around them.

I must mention that there is almost nothing new said in this book that hasn't been said earlier by me explicitly or implicitly. But a fresh attempt is made to explain the truth to the world in a more compact and effective way. The truth that the humanity must understand and appreciate! Probably one has no option but to go on trying till one perishes!!

One never knows if this will be my last such attempt. Even if so, I hope this book will achieve its purpose and will lead to an unprecedented awakening all around.

I do hope that there has not been a single false word from me in this book as has been the case with my various previous books and writings on Cricket, or in the writ petition filed by me in the Supreme Court of India on the subject. I just couldn't afford that, while taking single-handed on the rest of the big bad world😊. The readers will understand that the continuing crime through Cricket and sports does affect and should concern even those who are not cricket fans.

Since whether masses know it or not, the fact of cricket being what it is being beyond any question now (none other than Time has validated everything in 10 long years), the greater emphasis in this book will be on the implications of continuation of such an extraordinary crime. Hopefully, the readers will also be able to comprehend at last, despite the continuous camouflage, the reality of cricket. More than that, they will know the shocking and stunning implications!

An open mind and simple application of common sense on the part of the readers should suffice. And of course, they have to read this short book word by word.😊

I hope the readers won't mind some repetitions, resulting from the mention of the same things in different contexts. I also hope that such repetitions will help the readers in comprehending the reality better.

Thank you.

–Atul Kumar
October, 2023

An Overview of IPL-2023

The subject of crime and corruption in IPL and Cricket is as vast and deep as an ocean. To start with, let us have an overview of the scores and results of various matches of IPL-2023.

Mar 31, Fri
Chennai Super Kings vs Gujarat Titans, 1st Match
Narendra Modi Stadium, Ahmedabad
CSK 178/7
GT 182/5 (19.2 overs)
Gujarat Titans won by 5 wkts

Apr 01, Sat
Punjab Kings vs Kolkata Knight Riders, 2nd Match
Punjab Cricket Association IS Bindra Stadium, Mohali
PBKS 191/5
KKR 146/7 (16/16 overs, target 154)
Punjab Kings won by 7 runs (DLS method)

Lucknow Super Giants vs Delhi Capitals, 3rd Match
Bharat Ratna Shri Atal Bihari Vajpayee Ekana Cricket Stadium, Lucknow
LSG 193/6
DC 143/9
Lucknow Super Giants won by 50 runs

Apr 02, Sun

<u>Rajasthan Royals vs Sunrisers Hyderabad, 4th Match</u>
Rajiv Gandhi International Stadium, Hyderabad

RR	203/5
SRH	131/8

<u>Rajasthan Royals won by 72 runs</u>

<u>Mumbai Indians vs Royal Challengers Bangalore, 5th Match</u>
M.Chinnaswamy Stadium, Bengaluru

MI	171/7
RCB	172/2 (16.2 overs)

<u>Royal Challengers Bangalore won by 8 wkts</u>

Apr 03, Mon

<u>Chennai Super Kings vs Lucknow Super Giants, 6th Match</u>
MA Chidambaram Stadium, Chennai

CSK	217/7
LSG	205/7

<u>Chennai Super Kings won by 12 runs</u>

Apr 04, Tue

<u>Delhi Capitals vs Gujarat Titans, 7th Match</u>
Arun Jaitley Stadium, Delhi

DC	162/8
GT	163/4 (18.1 overs)

<u>Gujarat Titans won by 6 wkts</u>

Apr 05, Wed

<u>Punjab Kings vs Rajasthan Royals, 8th Match</u>
Barsapara Cricket Stadium, Guwahati

PBKS	197/4
RR	192/7

<u>Punjab Kings won by 5 runs</u>

Apr 06, Thu

Kolkata Knight Riders vs Royal Challengers Bangalore, 9th Match

Eden Gardens, Kolkata

KKR 204/7

RCB 123/10 (17.4 overs)

Kolkata Knight Riders won by 81 runs

Apr 07, Fri

Sunrisers Hyderabad vs Lucknow Super Giants, 10th Match

Bharat Ratna Shri Atal Bihari Vajpayee Ekana Cricket Stadium, Lucknow

SRH 121/8

LSG 127/5 (16 overs)

Lucknow Super Giants won by 5 wkts

Apr 08, Sat

Rajasthan Royals vs Delhi Capitals, 11th Match

Barsapara Cricket Stadium, Guwahati

RR 199/4

DC 142/9

Rajasthan Royals won by 57 runs

Mumbai Indians vs Chennai Super Kings, 12th Match

Wankhede Stadium, Mumbai

MI 157/8

CSK 159/3 (18.1 overs)

Chennai Super Kings won by 7 wkts

Apr 09, Sun

Gujarat Titans vs Kolkata Knight Riders, 13th Match

Narendra Modi Stadium, Ahmedabad

GT 204/4

KKR 207/7 (20 overs)

Kolkata Knight Riders won by 3 wkts

Punjab Kings vs Sunrisers Hyderabad, 14th Match
Rajiv Gandhi International Stadium, Hyderabad
PBKS 143/9
SRH 145/2 (17.1 overs)
Sunrisers Hyderabad won by 8 wkts

Apr 10, Mon
Royal Challengers Bangalore vs Lucknow Super Giants, 15th Match
M.Chinnaswamy Stadium, Bengaluru
RCB 212/2
LSG 213/9 (20 overs)
Lucknow Super Giants won by 1 wkt

Apr 11, Tue
Delhi Capitals vs Mumbai Indians, 16th Match
Arun Jaitley Stadium, Delhi
DC 172
MI 173/4 (20 overs)
Mumbai Indians won by 6 wkts

Apr 12, Wed
Rajasthan Royals vs Chennai Super Kings, 17th Match
MA Chidambaram Stadium, Chennai
RR 175/8
CSK 172/6
Rajasthan Royals won by 3 runs

Apr 13, Thu
Punjab Kings vs Gujarat Titans, 18th Match
Punjab Cricket Association IS Bindra Stadium, Mohali
PBKS 153/8
GT 154/4 (19.5 overs)
Gujarat Titans won by 6 wkts

Apr 14, Fri

Sunrisers Hyderabad vs Kolkata Knight Riders, 19th Match

Eden Gardens, Kolkata

SRH 228/4

KKR 205/7

Sunrisers Hyderabad won by 23 runs

Apr 15, Sat

Royal Challengers Bangalore vs Delhi Capitals, 20th Match

M.Chinnaswamy Stadium, Bengaluru

RCB 174/6

DC 151/9

Royal Challengers Bangalore won by 23 runs

Lucknow Super Giants vs Punjab Kings, 21st Match

Bharat Ratna Shri Atal Bihari Vajpayee Ekana Cricket Stadium, Lucknow

LSG 159/8

PBKS 161/8 (19.3 overs)

Punjab Kings won by 2 wkts

Apr 16, Sun

Kolkata Knight Riders vs Mumbai Indians, 22nd Match

Wankhede Stadium, Mumbai

KKR 185/6

MI 186/5 (17.4 overs)

Mumbai Indians won by 5 wkts

Gujarat Titans vs Rajasthan Royals, 23rd Match

Narendra Modi Stadium, Ahmedabad

GT 177/7

RR 179/7 (19.2 overs)

Rajasthan Royals won by 3 wkts

Apr 17, Mon

Chennai Super Kings vs Royal Challengers Bangalore, 24th Match

M.Chinnaswamy Stadium, Bengaluru

CSK 226/6

RCB 218/8

Chennai Super Kings won by 8 runs

Apr 18, Tue

Mumbai Indians vs Sunrisers Hyderabad, 25th Match

Rajiv Gandhi International Stadium, Hyderabad

MI 192/5

SRH 178/10 (19.5 overs)

Mumbai Indians won by 14 runs

Apr 19, Wed

Lucknow Super Giants vs Rajasthan Royals, 26th Match

Sawai Mansingh Stadium, Jaipur

LSG 154/7

RR 144/6

Lucknow Super Giants won by 10 runs

Apr 20, Thu

Royal Challengers Bangalore vs Punjab Kings, 27th Match

Punjab Cricket Association IS Bindra Stadium, Mohali

RCB 174/4

PBKS 150 (18.2 overs)

Royal Challengers Bangalore won by 24 runs

Kolkata Knight Riders vs Delhi Capitals, 28th Match

Arun Jaitley Stadium, Delhi

KKR 127

DC 128/6 (19.2 overs)

Delhi Capitals won by 4 wkts

Apr 21, Fri

Sunrisers Hyderabad vs Chennai Super Kings, 29th Match

MA Chidambaram Stadium, Chennai

SRH 134/7

CSK 138/3 (18.2 overs)

Chennai Super Kings won by 7 wkts

Apr 22, Sat

Gujarat Titans vs Lucknow Super Giants, 30th Match

Bharat Ratna Shri Atal Bihari Vajpayee Ekana Cricket Stadium, Lucknow

GT 135/6

LSG 128/7

Gujarat Titans won by 7 runs

Punjab Kings vs Mumbai Indians, 31st Match

Wankhede Stadium, Mumbai

PBKS 214/8

MI 201/6

Punjab Kings won by 13 runs

Apr 23, Sun

Royal Challengers Bangalore vs Rajasthan Royals, 32nd Match

M.Chinnaswamy Stadium, Bengaluru

RCB 189/9

RR 182/6

Royal Challengers Bangalore won by 7 runs

Chennai Super Kings vs Kolkata Knight Riders, 33rd Match

Eden Gardens, Kolkata

CSK 235/4

KKR 186/8

Chennai Super Kings won by 49 runs

Apr 24, Mon

Delhi Capitals vs Sunrisers Hyderabad, 34th Match

Rajiv Gandhi International Stadium, Hyderabad

DC	144/9
SRH	137/6

Delhi Capitals won by 7 runs

Apr 25, Tue

Gujarat Titans vs Mumbai Indians, 35th Match

Narendra Modi Stadium, Ahmedabad

GT	207/6
MI	152/9

Gujarat Titans won by 55 runs

Apr 26, Wed

Kolkata Knight Riders vs Royal Challengers Bangalore, 36th Match

M.Chinnaswamy Stadium, Bengaluru

KKR	200/5
RCB	179/8

Kolkata Knight Riders won by 21 runs

Apr 27, Thu

Rajasthan Royals vs Chennai Super Kings, 37th Match

Sawai Mansingh Stadium, Jaipur

RR	202/5
CSK	170/6

Rajasthan Royals won by 32 runs

Apr 28, Fri

Lucknow Super Giants vs Punjab Kings, 38th Match

Punjab Cricket Association IS Bindra Stadium, Mohali

LSG	257/5
PBKS	201 (19.5 overs)

Lucknow Super Giants won by 56 runs

Apr 29, Sat

Kolkata Knight Riders vs Gujarat Titans, 39th Match

Eden Gardens, Kolkata

KKR 179/7

GT 180/3 (17.5 overs)

Gujarat Titans won by 7 wkts

Sunrisers Hyderabad vs Delhi Capitals, 40th Match

Arun Jaitley Stadium, Delhi

SRH 197/6

DC 188/6

Sunrisers Hyderabad won by 9 runs

Apr 30, Sun

Chennai Super Kings vs Punjab Kings, 41st Match

MA Chidambaram Stadium, Chennai

CSK 200/4

PBKS 201/6 (20 overs)

Punjab Kings won by 4 wkts

Rajasthan Royals vs Mumbai Indians, 42nd Match

Wankhede Stadium, Mumbai

RR 212/7

MI 214/4 (19.3 overs)

Mumbai Indians won by 6 wkts

May 1, Mon

Royal Challengers Bangalore vs Lucknow Super Giants, 43rd Match

Bharat Ratna Shri Atal Bihari Vajpayee Ekana Cricket Stadium, Lucknow

RCB 126/9

LSG 108 (19.5 overs)

Royal Challengers Bangalore won by 18 runs

May 02, Tue

Delhi Capitals vs Gujarat Titans, 44th Match

Narendra Modi Stadium, Ahmedabad

DC 130/8

GT 125/6

Delhi Capitals won by 5 runs

May 03, Wed

Lucknow Super Giants vs Chennai Super Kings, 45th Match

Bharat Ratna Shri Atal Bihari Vajpayee Ekana Cricket Stadium, Lucknow

LSG 125/7 (19.2/20 overs)

CSK

No result (washed out)

Punjab Kings vs Mumbai Indians, 46th Match

Punjab Cricket Association IS Bindra Stadium, Mohali

PBKS 214/3

MI 216/4 (18.5 overs)

Mumbai Indians won by 6 wkts

May 04, Thu

Kolkata Knight Riders vs Sunrisers Hyderabad, 47th Match

Rajiv Gandhi International Stadium, Hyderabad

KKR 171/9

SRH 166/8

Kolkata Knight Riders won by 5 runs

May 05, Fri

Rajasthan Royals vs Gujarat Titans, 48th Match

Sawai Mansingh Stadium, Jaipur

RR 118

GT 119/1 (13.5 overs)

Gujarat Titans won by 9 wkts

May 06, Sat

Mumbai Indians vs Chennai Super Kings, 49th Match

MA Chidambaram Stadium, Chennai

MI 139/8

CSK 140/4 (17.4 overs)

Chennai Super Kings won by 6 wkts

Royal Challengers Bangalore vs Delhi Capitals, 50th Match

Arun Jaitley Stadium, Delhi

RCB 181/4

DC 187/3 (16.4 overs)

Delhi Capitals won by 7 wkts

May 07, Sun

Gujarat Titans vs Lucknow Super Giants, 51st Match

Narendra Modi Stadium, Ahmedabad

GT 227/2

LSG 171/7

Gujarat Titans won by 56 runs

Rajasthan Royals vs Sunrisers Hyderabad, 52nd Match

Sawai Mansingh Stadium, Jaipur

RR 214/2

SRH 217/6 (20 overs)

Sunrisers Hyderabad won by 4 wkts

May 08, Mon

Kolkata Knight Riders vs Punjab Kings, 53rd Match

Eden Gardens, Kolkata

PBKS 179/7

KKR 182/5 (20 overs)

Kolkata Knight Riders won by 5 wkts

May 09, Tue

Mumbai Indians vs Royal Challengers Bangalore, 54th Match

Wankhede Stadium, Mumbai

RCB	199/6
MI	200/4 (16.3 overs)

Mumbai Indians won by 6 wkts

May 10, Wed

Chennai Super Kings vs Delhi Capitals, 55th Match

MA Chidambaram Stadium, Chennai

CSK	167/8
DC	140/8

Chennai Super Kings won by 27 runs

May 11, Thu

Kolkata Knight Riders vs Rajasthan Royals, 56th Match

Eden Gardens, Kolkata

KKR	149/8
RR	151/1 (13.1 overs)

Rajasthan Royals won by 9 wkts

May 12, Fri

Mumbai Indians vs Gujarat Titans, 57th Match

Wankhede Stadium, Mumbai

MI	218/5
GT	191/8

Mumbai Indians won by 27 runs

May 13, Sat

Sunrisers Hyderabad vs Lucknow Super Giants, 58th Match

Rajiv Gandhi International Stadium, Hyderabad

SRH	182/6
LSG	185/3 (19.2 overs)

Lucknow Super Giants won by 7 wkts

Delhi Capitals vs Punjab Kings, 59th Match
Arun Jaitley Stadium, Delhi
PBKS 167/7
DC 136/8
Punjab Kings won by 31 runs

May 14, Sun
Rajasthan Royals vs Royal Challengers Bangalore, 60th Match
Sawai Mansingh Stadium, Jaipur
RCB 171/5
RR 59 (10.3 overs)
Royal Challengers Bangalore won by 112 runs

Chennai Super Kings vs Kolkata Knight Riders, 61st Match
MA Chidambaram Stadium, Chennai
CSK 144/6
KKR 147/4 (18.3 overs)
Kolkata Knight Riders won by 6 wkts

May 15, Mon
Gujarat Titans vs Sunrisers Hyderabad, 62nd Match
Narendra Modi Stadium, Ahmedabad
GT 188/9
SRH 154/9
Gujarat Titans won by 34 runs

May 16, Tue
Lucknow Super Giants vs Mumbai Indians, 63rd Match
Bharat Ratna Shri Atal Bihari Vajpayee Ekana Cricket Stadium, Lucknow
LSG 177/3
MI 172/5
Lucknow Super Giants won by 5 runs

May 17, Wed

Punjab Kings vs Delhi Capitals, 64th Match

Himachal Pradesh Cricket Association Stadium, Dharamsala

DC	213/2
PBKS	198/8

Delhi Capitals won by 15 runs

May 18, Thu

Sunrisers Hyderabad vs Royal Challengers Bangalore, 65th Match

Rajiv Gandhi International Stadium, Hyderabad

SRH	186/5
RCB	187/2 (19.2 overs)

Royal Challengers Bangalore won by 8 wkts

May 19, Fri

Punjab Kings vs Rajasthan Royals, 66th Match

Himachal Pradesh Cricket Association Stadium, Dharamsala

PBKS	187/5
RR	189/6

Rajasthan Royals won by 4 wkts

May 20, Sat

Delhi Capitals vs Chennai Super Kings, 67th Match

Arun Jaitley Stadium, Delhi

CSK	223/3
DC	146/9

Chennai Super Kings won by 77 runs

Kolkata Knight Riders vs Lucknow Super Giants, 68th Match

Eden Gardens, Kolkata

LSG	176/8
KKR	175/7

Lucknow Super Giants won by 1 run

May 21, Sun

<u>Mumbai Indians Vs Sunrisers Hyderabad, 69th Match</u>

Wankhede Stadium, Mumbai

SRH	200/5
MI	201/2 (18 overs)

Mumbai Indians won by 8 wkts

<u>Royal Challengers Bangalore vs Gujarat Titans, 70th Match</u>

M.Chinnaswamy Stadium, Bengaluru

RCB	197/5
GT	198/4 (19.1 overs)

Gujarat Titans won by 6 wkts

May 23, Tue

Gujarat Titans vs Chennai Super Kings, Qualifier 1

MA Chidambaram Stadium, Chennai

CSK	172/7
GT	157 (20 overs)

Chennai Super Kings won by 15 runs

May 24, Wed

<u>Lucknow Super Giants vs Mumbai Indians, Eliminator</u>

MA Chidambaram Stadium, Chennai

MI	182/8
LSG	101 (16.3 overs)

Mumbai Indians won by 81 runs

May 26, Fri

<u>Gujarat Titans vs Mumbai Indians, Qualifier 2</u>

Narendra Modi Stadium, Ahmedabad

GT	233/3
MI	171 (18.3 overs)

Gujarat Titans won by 62 runs

May 28, Sun
Chennai Super Kings vs Gujarat Titans, Final
Narendra Modi Stadium, Ahmedabad
Match postponed to Monday due to rain

May 29, Mon
Chennai Super Kings vs Gujarat Titans, Final (Reserve Day)
Narendra Modi Stadium, Ahmedabad
GT 214/4 (20 overs)
CSK 171/5 (15/15 overs, target 171)
Mumbai Indians won by 5 wkts

These scores and results as such don't tell anything and don't prove anything. These give us only some statistical data. Such as, 10 of the 73 completed matches (1wash out) were decided on the last ball - matches numbers 13, 15, 16, 17, 41, 44, 47, 52, 53, and the Final; 45% or so matches were decided in the last over of the match; 200 or more runs were scored in as many as 37 innings; out of 12 less than 150 scores, 4 were defended; 170 or more were scored in as many as 94 innings etc. etc. These and other statistics are only statistics, these don't form any proof for scripting or fixing of matches. Though, these do give an overview of the scripting of the matches in IPL-2023.

When we open our eyes and start to think about strange/ self-defeating behaviour/performance of batters and bowlers, especially in crucial stages of these matches, supposed to be do or die battles, and further apply common sense, the things start becoming clear. We shall see that as we move on.

Necessary to repeat here that above will be over and above the fact that ball-by-ball scripting of such matches lies publicly exposed and scientifically established for more than a decade.

Such a colossal fraud and crime continuing unfettered for 10 long years after having been publicly exposed is no small matter. But for the infinite stupidity of the human race (none other than one of the greatest scientists ever, Albert Einstein, said so about a century back), as we would see in a subsequent chapter, it just couldn't continue and prosper as it has been doing! The fact has not been disputed by anyone, by ICC or anyone else, for more than 10 long years. Nothing was disputed by any authority even when the averment to this effect was made in the Supreme Court of India more than 5 years back. The people at large don't know much because the powerful Media keeps them deceived as mentioned in the preface.

Opening Eyes to IPL-2023

I reproduce the following forward I received in one of my Whatsapp groups around 10th May, 2023:

'IPL is utter nonsense

I've been watching most of the IPL highlights in kayo, and it often looks like the games are played to a script of sorts. There are far more pace on half-volleys and full tosses bowled than elite fast bowlers should be bowling in the death overs. Do any of you think that the players are being instructed in some situations to make it a close finish by giving the batting team easy runs?

As an example from the most recent match, in the penultimate over, Sam Curran bowled multiple half-volleys on Andre Russell's pads that he whipped away for boundaries. I think Curran's skillset is good enough to execute a bit better than that. Also, in an earlier game, Jason Holder bowled 3 consecutive full tosses to Tim David when Mumbai needed 17 from the last over, and David hit them all for 6. Going back a bit further, when Rinku Singh hit 5 sixes in the last over for victory, they were all terrible deliveries.'

So, some eyes have started opening at last. Though very few eyes are opening very little! The masses at large continue to be titillated by 4's and 6's and last ball and last over finishes. They are just not bothered what was happening why. They are hundreds of millions of people, including thousands of intellectuals and

professionals. They are mostly not aware or care two hoots that the same titillating matches had been scripted to turn tens of millions of their betting brethren broke. They simply feel happy with their thrills and titillations.

And those tens of millions of bettors/punters turning broke sooner or later are not bothered either. They are mostly the addicted lot, whose only motto in life has become to bet again and again in an attempt to win/earn easy money. Mostly they continue to bet in a hope to recover the lost amounts, losing even more in the bargain. They just don't worry about the huge implications of the humungous crime that openly goes on and on. They are worried only about winning or losing in betting. **If that were not so, M S Dhoni, Virat Kohli & company wouldn't being worshipped like demigods, but would being tried and jailed as top criminals under public pressure.**

Let us apply our mind to some more plays during IPL-2023, other than very few mentioned in the above Whatsapp message. Let us go to the 43rd match played between LSG and RCB. LSG required only 127 runs to win, but were all out for 108. Only in their last match they had scored the highest score, 257, of IPL-2023. Their main batsman, captain Rahul came to bat only at number 11, though he was being shown in readiness to come to bat after 5th wicket fell or thereabouts. The last ball of the 19th over he faced turned out be a no ball. He made absolutely no attempt to hit the resulting free hit ball for a 4 or 6. Rather he meekly tapped the ball straight to a fielder, thus not even getting strike in the last over. There can't be any cricketing explanation to that! Here we are not talking of any tom, dick, and harry, but of Rahul, of someone having the capability he possesses, of a top batter of the dreaded Indian XI. Still, some would try to dismiss it saying, 'oh! He was injured and came to bat only as a formality.'

In the 17th match between RR and CSK, CSK required 40 runs of last 2 overs, a seemingly very difficult job, with their match-winners Dhoni and Jadeja on the crease. They did get 33 runs of first 9 out of those 12 balls. When everyone thought that it was now CSK's game, the last 3 balls were inexplicably played for 3 singles. One can watch the replay of the match to assimilate how the match winners played those 3 balls to lose the match, not trying at all to win it. It looked so absurd on the very face of it that it prompted me to write the facebook post https://www.facebook.com/atulrailway/posts/pfbid0E96Khfb-PYm3tNie5QueM24mN463CxpM7e6vp7F8o9NCm2jGN4vst-w6bLQQK5Xv5Yl on 13/4/2023:

'B for Billion; B for Blind

The tense faces in the cricket stadiums, people biting nails, unmindful that what they were seeing was only a staged drama, thoroughly brainwashed to the contrary by the cricketers, the commentators, the cricket journalists, the cricket experts, and all other marketeers of the mega fraud round the clock; makes one marvel at the blindness of the billions of humans across the globe.

One wonders, how come the cricket fans are too blind to see that everything is a staged drama even when seeing batsmen or bowlers suddenly change gears to lose a match wilfully, match after match. Like very well-set Dhoni and Jadeja hitting sixes at will till then, requiring only 7 runs of last 3 balls, chose to play those 3 balls for 3 singles, with even no intent to hit a six or a four, in the CSK vs RR match of IPL-16 yesterday, to lose the match!!'

Let us come straight to the final of the IPL-2023 now. Something in total contrast happened here. Chasing 171 to win in 15 overs (applying DLS), CSK required 38 runs in last

3 overs or 18 balls. Ambati Rayudu scored 16 runs of first 3 of those balls, only 22 were required of the last 15 balls now. Suddenly 2 wickets fell off consecutive deliveries, the great Dhoni going for golden duck. Still CSK required only 21 runs of last 2 overs, with their 6 hitter of the season Shivam Dubey and Jadeja on the crease. The two played the first 10 of those 12 balls, for 11 laborious runs only, totally against their capability, and contrary to built-up reputation, leaving 10 runs for last 2 balls. And exactly a 6 and a 4 were consecutively hit of those two balls. How could Jadeja or CSK be sure of achieving that, to have dragged the match to that stage from a very comfortable winning position after 12.3 overs? Why would a bowler in his rhythm suddenly bowl rank bad balls to lose the coveted final? How that sudden topsy-turviness would have baffled the tens of millions of punters around the globe and earned huge profits for the betting syndicates/mafia!! **The more the punters are caught on the wrong foot, through unthinkable twists or through unthinkable collapses of teams or through absurdly one-sided matches otherwise, the more the betting mafia stands to gain.**

But, for the masses, CSK had done it and Jadeja and Dhoni were the super heroes!! The masses neither understood what was happening nor wanted to understand anything. They were just happy with the thrills! If some mind-boggling fraud was taking place in front of their very own eyes, they were not supposed to know and bother. They were supposed to bother only about petty wrong-doings and crimes around them and to make a lot of noise about those on social media or otherwise!! Throughout their lives they had been tutored so and their minds had been conditioned thus!! The mob mentality ruled.

Let us go back to two consecutive matches involving SRH, match numbers 47 and 52. In the 47th match against KKR,

chasing 172 to win, SRH were well placed at 124/4 after 14 overs, with their two main batsmen Klassen and Markram well set. Then Klassen suddenly got out, finishing his given role for the day (see the shot and you would understand). At the time of second strategic time out, SRH were still in the driver's seat, requiring only 38 runs from 30 balls with 5 good wickets still in hand. One can easily see how SRH batted from thereon to lose the match by 5 runs, even though they required only 9 runs of the last over. Not that such a thing can't happen in natural cricket, but one with an open mind can easily see how most of the last 30 balls were played by the batsmen showing lack of intention/efforts to win the match! Something that Bishan Singh Bedi indicated in 2018.

While SRH lost this match out of nowhere, they won their very next match, the match number 52 against RR, out of nowhere. They won requiring 41 runs of last 2 overs or 12 balls. It was that extraordinarily dramatic match. They appeared to have lost when suddenly it was revealed that the last ball bowled was a no ball. From the resulting free hit, 6 was hit and SRH won a lost match! Was it Cricket or some new extraordinary script being played? One may see or one may not see; but to remind the readers, the fact of cricket/IPL being thoroughly scripted remains a foregone conclusion. Mr Suresh Menon, the veteran sports journalist, were to comment too ignorantly on this (as we shall see in a later chapter).

Then one may also revisit the eliminator between LSG and MI, played on the 24th May, 2023. Chasing 183 to win, LSG were well in contention at 65/2 after the 7th over. Then they suddenly decided to go into shell and lose the match pretty soon through hara-kiri, the suicidal run-outs being too obvious. I am sure one will find it difficult to believe that those run-outs of the well trained and highly experienced professionals of

repute were result of any natural happening. A very sudden collapse, no one could imagine of. Cricket can be by chance, but how often? The intentional hara-kiri by players (batters or bowlers or fielders)/teams, not rare or uncommon at all, is another matter, and can easily be seen by an open mind, at least at times.

Let us pause here and think what Cricket is. Cricket is a game, a sport, essentially a function of bowling. A bowler bowls a ball independent of anything, and what follows is a function of the bowled ball. A ball is bowled, then the batsman plays the shot depending on that ball, and then the fielding etc. (if the batsman does not get *out*, bowled or lbw). Any cricket match can be severed into distinct balls; first a ball is bowled and then the rest of action takes place for that ball.

A match is supposed to be played to win by the two teams. The players at show in IPL are highly talented and extremely trained ones. The viewers are ordinary mortals, most of them don't know much about the nitty-gritties of the game. They view a match from their level of knowledge/perception, as some unfolding drama. So, they either fail to see when the accomplished bowlers purposefully bowl loose or wide or no balls (acting out their given role or as a puppet), or they simply don't bother. Similarly, the well-set batsmen won't play atrocious shots, mostly hits aimed straight to the fielders for getting caught out, as often as we see, especially exactly at a moment when match appeared to be for the taking for the batting team (happens quite often), if they were playing naturally – to win. But the thousands of viewers, especially in the grounds, are not concerned with all this. They just enjoy the drama, the thrill, and the atmosphere, while biting their nails during those last over and last ball finishes.

Some plays do appear palpably fishy at some point of time in this match or that match to a very casual viewer also, even when one doesn't have the least idea that it all was scripted. But one forgets and gets engaged in subsequent plays very quickly. And if one watches the matches, with grey cells working, one can quite often see these dubious happenings many times a day across matches. That is because now-a-days, simultaneously many matches are played on the same day, in various leagues or international matches. One can very often see bowlers/batsmen/fielders performing to lose on purpose (never mind the articles by naïve journalists like Suresh Menon).

Let us try to briefly look at some more matches of IPL 2023, including some matches picked at random, before proceeding further.

Let us go to the 31st match between Punjab Kings (PBKS) and Mumbai Indians (MI), played at Wankhede stadium, Mumbai on the 22nd April, 2023. It would appear to be a normal match to any casual viewer. MI won the toss and decided to field first. PBKS scored 214/8 in the allotted 20 overs, and MI ended at 201/6 while chasing the target, losing the match by 13 runs. PBKS scored 17 runs in the last over, even though 2 wickets fell; while only 2 runs in the 10th over. They scored 13 and 12 runs in the 15th and the 6th over respectively. I mention these overs because these were the last overs for the sessions of 6 overs, 10 overs, 15 overs and the 20 overs. A lot of betting across the globe, in millions and billions of dollars, takes place for the ultimate score at the end of these sessions. One can easily see that other than normal scoring took place in these overs. It won't necessarily be so always, but quite often it is so.

Overall, it was a very normal looking score line; but in this match also every wicket fell and every run was scored at the

dictates of some betting mafia/ betting syndicate, exactly as Sanjeev Chawla had told a couple of years ago. While those having necessary cricketing acumen can see that from the balls bowled / shots played during the match, especially at crucial junctures, the others should be able to grasp the same from the contents of the next chapter.

https://www.timesnownews.com/sports/cricket/article/no-cricket-match-is-fairly-played-all-are-fixed-sanjeev-chawla-accused-bookie-hansie-cronje-fixing-scandal/599061 brings out who Sanjeev Chawla is and what he had said in end May, 2020:

"In February this year, bookie Sanjeev Chawla was brought back to India from the UK after an exile of two decades. The bookie was allegedly a part of one of the biggest match-fixing scandals that India witnessed in 2000 when the Hansie Cronje-led South African team had toured the sub-continent.

Recordings of his conversation with the late Proteas skipper exposed arguably the biggest corruption scandal in Indian cricket. Having chased him for nearly 20 years, the police managed to bring the 50-year-old back to India after completing formalities of his extradition from a UK court at the beginning of the year. While the investigation has been ongoing, Chawla has made a shocking statement by suggesting that no cricket match played at the professional level is 100% fair.

"No cricket match is fairly played. All the cricket matches which people see are fixed", he was quoted as saying by Indian Express. Chawla further spoke of the involvement of "a very big syndicate/underworld mafia" that controls what happens in the cricket game, just like "movies which are already being directed by someone".

As per the report in the paper, Chawla revealed to the police the underworld mafia has the case's investigation officer DCP (Crime Branch) Dr G Ram Gopal Naik on his target and his life is under threat.

Chawla, who is a London-based bookmaker born in New Delhi, has admitted to have fixed matches on several occasions. He, however, refused to delve into further details as the underworld mafia he works with could get him killed.

"A very big syndicate/underworld mafia is involved in this matter and they are dangerous people and if he says anything they will get him killed," he said.

In another statement to the police, Chawla revealed that the other accused in the case - Krishan Kumar, Rajesh Kalra, and Sunil Dara - were his old friends who were also involved in fixing matches."

Let us see the 15th match, between RCB and LSG. Batting first, RCB scored imposing 212/2. While chasing, LSG were in a hopeless condition at 23/3 in 4 overs. From there, they came to a comfortable winning position at 189/5. Just when the match appeared in their grip, a sudden collapse started before they won on the last ball scoring 213/9.

In the 41st match between CSK and PBKS played at Chennai, considered to be the fortress of CSK, CSK scored a high score of 200/4 for that ground. And yet, their dreaded bowling couldn't defend it, PBKS winning by scoring 3 runs on the last ball. What the punters least expected, happened.

Serving exactly such a purpose, in the 44th match, the lowly placed DC went on to beat the table toppers GT after being 23/5.

Here is the match report, https://www.espncricinfo.com/series/indian-premier-league-2023-1345038/gujarat-titans-vs-delhi-capitals-44th-match-1359518/match-report :

*'**Delhi Capitals** 130 for 8 (Aman 51, Shami 4-11, Mohit 2-33) beat **Gujarat Titans** 125 for 6 (Hardik 59*, Ishant 2-23, Khaleel 2-24) by five runs*

In a game with twists of epic proportions, tenth-placed Delhi Capitals trumped table-toppers Gujarat Titans in Ahmedabad, winning by five runs in dramatic fashion.

The game's pendulum swung numerous times, starting with Mohammed Shami picking up four wickets inside the powerplay to reduce Capitals to 23 for 5. But Aman Hakim Khan's maiden T20 fifty and contributions from Axar Patel and Ripal Patel dragged the Capitals to 130 for 8.

Capitals then took the upper hand when Khaleel Ahmed, Ishant Sharma and Kuldeep Yadav left the Titans on the mat at 32 for 4. Even though Hardik Pandya steadied the chase with a half-century, the momentum was with Capitals going into the final two overs.

Just when the game seemed lost, Rahul Tewatia hit a hat-trick of sixes off Anrich Nortje in the 19th over to bring Titans to within touching distance of victory. But Ishant held his nerve in the final over and conceded just six against Hardik, Tewatia and Rashid Khan to seal the deal for Capitals.'

We can go on and on with match after match. We can see unnatural cricket in all the matches through the balls bowled by accomplished bowlers and the shots played by the accomplished batters, through the timing of big hits or wickets, bad balls or

good balls, if we don't choose to be blind, and don't want to see only what the commentators or the mafia want us to see!

All the matches of IPL-2023 were "just like movies which are already being directed by someone," exactly as Sanjeev Chawla had told a few years ago.

❐

It's elementary, My dear Watson!

We get governed by beliefs deeply ingrained in us. For example, we, the humans, belonging to the same species, have different religious beliefs. The advantages and disadvantages of these beliefs will always remain debatable. As long as these beliefs lead us to the same truth, it may be alright; but there must be something wrong if the differing beliefs lead us to confrontation amongst us.

We must agree and accept that beliefs are beliefs, there is nothing scientific about them. We may accredit something to be scientific when it applies equally to all, and is not subjective. The most of the things we are taught under 'moral science' are common beliefs we all must follow for a peaceful and happy co-existence.

But unfortunately, the human world is not ruled by saints. If it were not so, there won't be wars and the occurrence of humans exploiting and killing humans. The forces controlling the world know very well that nothing but mob mentality has always governed the egoist humans (howsoever wise they may think themselves to be), and will always govern them. To achieve their nefarious purposes, these forces have ensured and seen to it that some totally wrong or false beliefs remain deeply ingrained in the masses.

One such belief deeply ingrained in us for many decades is that '**sporadic fixing takes place sometimes in some cricket matches by some misguided/corrupt players at the behest of some bookies.**' Tens of films/series, fiction or non-fiction, have been churned out on the subject over the years, out of ignorance or on purpose, and have bombarded our consciousness repeatedly. Apart from other purposes, all these have served the purpose of reinforcing us, the masses, with the above false/wrong belief. '**Caught Out**' is probably the latest such documentary screened for the whole world by the OTT platform, Netflix. Earlier, the much more popular fictional series '**Inside Edge**' on Amazon Prime served this purpose. Many movies like *Jannat* (Hindi movie) also have been contributing vastly to this wrong belief for decades.

Here it is worth noting that the technologically very advanced 21st century world had been accepting and hailing these expressions of utter falsehood even when the truth was in its full knowledge since 2013 as a result of my efforts. This is how not truth but falsehood and mob mentality continue to govern our species. Probably, my facebook post https://www.facebook.com/atulrailway/posts/pfbid02mh6GWyFhUxtEQAprEh7bbW5kwsjic4ixfry3coGzC6PcG2erdzmHZPWHrctwwSN8l dated 15th April, 2023 sums this up. I reproduce it here for ready reference and record:

'Caught Out on Netflix by Supriya Sobti Gupta:

Just now finished watching the documentary film. I won't say it's a bad film per se; but it's relevance today was a bit baffling to me. And more baffling was the height of ignorance of the film maker about the subject.

The film is like someone talking today about times of postcard/inland letters, not at all aware of any of the

technological progressions that have taken place since then. The moneys involved, the depth and breadth of corruption and fixing, the Cricket itself (with the advent of leagues all around the world), the people involved - all has changed by leaps and bounds over last two decades. I know for sure, some of the characters shown in the film on the right side of law, journalists as well as from police, themselves have been protecting the wrong-doings in recent times.

Such films do a great disservice to the humanity. These keep people, the billions, fooled and totally ignorant of the reality. The reality is reality, howsoever incomprehensible or mind-boggling/unbelievable it is. thecricketmafia.com refers.

Today, it is crystal clear that fixing is throughout, from first ball till the end of any match, everything is institutional, the ICC itself controlling the thorough fixing of cricket. The investigations or journalistic adventurism shown in this documentary are all meaningless and irrelevant. Today, all the authorities themselves are part and parcel of the mega fraud called Cricket that gets necessary protection from none other than the honourable Supreme Court of India. Today, the anti-corruption bodies, of ICC or of cricket boards or outside cricket boards are all an eye-wash, a farce.😩😩

More than a decade ago, it could be termed as a good film, but today overall it can only be termed horrible; given the reality of it all that is already in the public domain for a decade and well in knowledge of some of the journalists who are posing big in this very film.😔’

Much more than these film makers, our coveted media, hardly anyone excluded, has been reinforcing this false belief through periodical stories of sporadic fixing or spot fixing brought to us. And there are and have been many other forces doing the same.

For one, the concocted, planted, or misleading stories like https://m.timesofindia.com/sports/cricket/ipl/top-stories/ipl-2023-mohammed-siraj-reports-corrupt-approach-to-bcci-acu/articleshow/99604823.cms continue reinforcing this totally false notion in our mind.

It is this deeply ingrained belief into our psyche, irrespective of our religion or country, that has been keeping our minds blocked, keeping us blinded, and not letting us see the truth which can easily be understood with a little application of commonsense - we all are supposed to be endowed with.

As we have seen in the last chapter, one did come across many plays in the matches of IPL 2023 that essentially were not natural cricket, were fishy, self-defeating, and/or inexplicable. And one does come across many such plays daily in various matches of cricket one views on TV. I give a very simple example here. Please visit the instances of 'free hit' balls resulting from no-balls bowled in various such matches over the years, and you will be shocked to see that most of those were not hit as one would have expected or as the batters must have hit those or at least must have attempted to hit in a limited overs match where one can't let go any opportunity to score. There are hundreds of such balls that one can see. And then of course there are many instances every day, of batsmen wilfully playing atrocious shots to get out, or well accomplished bowlers bowling atrocious balls. Many instances of run-outs and missed run-outs amply show the hara-kiri or coordination among the batters and the fielders to achieve the end result, to any discerning eye. Without going into other details, one clearly sees or can see many instances of unnatural cricket daily.

Can these instances be manifestation of sporadic or spot fixing? By some misguided players, at the behest of some

bookies? If that were so, won't the coaches, the managers, and the reputed cricket experts thoroughly monitoring these matches take any action? Will they keep quiet? Can these obviously suicidal plays by the players in the cricket grounds escape their hawk-eyes or scrutiny? That too, when we, the normal viewers, can see everything!

While such mockery of Cricket continues round the clock, same players continue to play in many leagues or international matches, without ever being questioned by any authority in cricket or outside, by anyone. That necessarily means that everything is institutionalised, and all the talk by all of spot or sporadic fixing over the years is a big hogwash. That hogwash has purposefully been created by the rogue-forces to keep you and me, the masses, fooled. In today's world, with all actions of all the players in the ground being always under the lens, no player can afford to be mischievous on his/her own, without having to pay a heavy price. I don't deny that many people contributing to the hogwash may have just been plain idiots (with their thoroughly conditioned and blocked minds), like many cricket journalists, and not a part of the rogue-forces.

Let us see the whole thing from another angle. Let us say, that out of hundreds of matches we see, just one ball is definitely fishy/ unnatural/ fixed. Can one ball be fixed in isolation? Won't this one ball have the potential of affecting the end result? And why on earth will someone fix just one ball? Can same set of players play fixed cricket at times and natural cricket at other times in the same match? Will they do so? Does it make any sense? **Saying that only a part of a match was fishy/ fixed amounts to saying that there was a partial story without there being the whole story of which it was a part.**😊😊 There just can't be spot fixing or sporadic fixing alone in a cricket match.

That doesn't make any sense. Either the whole match is fixed or there is no fixing/ fishy play whatsoever. It's elementary.

Extending the same logic, only one match or a few matches of a series or league or a competition can't be fixed. The result of any one match would affect the result of the whole tournament or the bilateral series. Same teams playing some matches fixed and fiercely competing in others doesn't make any sense, or does it? Even otherwise, how can even one fixed match be played in the open with the authorities taking no action? Either no fixed match ever takes place or the authorities are hand-in-glove. Again, elementary!

There can be and have been cases of some players trying to act extra smart within an already institutionally fixed match. They are then caught by the authorities and brought to book. What happens is that the people just vaguely talk or think of fixing, without bothering to apply mind/ common-sense to the facts and the possibilities.

Let us revisit the final over of the final of IPL 2023. It just couldn't be that only final over or a couple of final overs were scripted. For the match to come to that stage, it was necessary that scripting before that also had been done. **A story can't have only the last para.** Again, very elementary!

This chapter doesn't mean to prove anything. An encyclopaedia of evidence already exists. The scientific evidence exists for 10 years now. **The world continuing to be blind to something can't and doesn't neutralize its existence**. There is hardly anything new said in this chapter related to Cricket that has not been said earlier by me in my earlier writings.

Yet, this chapter certainly is intended to help the readers understand the reality of IPL-2023 and of Cricket in general

without much efforts; without having to know about betting (all fixing necessarily revolves around betting) and having to go through the existing mathematical/scientific evidence, the details of the PIL on the subject in the Supreme Court of India and its aftermath (all lying thoroughly documented in the book 'We the Oodles') or my earlier writings on the subject etc.

Any reasonably intelligent reader will appreciate that no one can deny something proved scientifically. Rest all has to follow. Also, when even the mighty Supreme Court of India chooses to stand exposed and publicly defenceless about/on an issue, losing its credibility for ever, rather than doing its duty, only ignorant, die-hard fools and/or crooks will have any doubts about the authenticity of what is what. It must have had some very strong compulsions to act such that the mafia remained protected!

I am sure, any normally intelligent viewer does come across many palpably absurd plays in the ground very frequently every day (once he/she chooses to apply mind also to what is on view), whether it be small or big leagues or international matches; such that the existence of natural cricket gets totally ruled out. Now let us try to remember the famous quote of Sherlock Holmes, *"How often have I said to you that when you have eliminated the impossible, whatever remains, however improbable, must be the truth?"* Application of common-sense as brought out above, and the very existence of session betting in Cricket, both independent of each other, tell us that it's impossible that most of the cricket matches (necessarily all the big tournaments at least) available for betting were not scripted ball-by-ball (or almost so). There also are a lot of other things/evidence to support it.

Since the players are always only acting out their given role for the day in the cricket grounds, whether very big names in international matches or relatively unknown players in state

leagues; there can't be anything like form of a player that comes into play. Through ignorant or idiotic/rogue commentators or journalists, this non-existent thing lies deeply and wrongly ingrained in our minds. Similarly, no external factors like pitch, weather, dew etc. ever affect the outcome of a match, since that is scripted by the cricket/betting mafia. Yes, these factors can always be taken into account while writing / deciding upon the script of a match.

The breath-taking catches, instances of extra-ordinarily good fielding, or silly doings, decisions by umpires and third umpires etc. – everything has to be scripted, howsoever improbable the same may appear to be. Some aberrations are bound to take place while executing the script or some random balls may be provided for in the script (in order to counter some shaky superficial questioners) now and then, to be taken care of in the subsequent plays.

This is no small crime, where hundreds of gentlemanly cricketers, the top political and corporate leaders, the law-enforcers, vast media, all the cricket boards and ICC, and many more join hands. So don't feel surprised that the on-field reviews and decisions by third umpires with the help of technology etc., everything is rigged/ pre-decided. **It has to be.**

The commentators also play a big role in this crime. Through their commentary, they create a world of make-believe by giving cricketing logic to the plays in the grounds, when in fact only puppet shows were taking place. They assist the crime in a big way by assisting in keeping the crime camouflaged. In addition, they also purposefully mislead the punters/bettors (those who place bets on cricket matches) at times, like tipsters, as agents of the mafia. I have given many examples in my previous writings.

Can there be anything inexplicable? Not only we ourselves come across many inexplicable actions (of batting, bowling, or fielding) by many seasoned players, but at times even the commentators also pronounce something as inexplicable and just proceed on. No one pauses to think. There has to be some explanation somewhere, and only plausible explanation for seemingly inexplicable frequent plays/actions one comes across is that there was no natural cricket, only a puppet show was taking place.

The incidents of batsmen given out lbw after having edged the ball, or wicketkeepers standing close to wicket and catching an edge off the bat but batsmen not given out, and reviews not taken though available to the players at the receiving end, can be termed inexplicable. Especially when the players can be seen taking absurd reviews often. The complicity of the umpires has to be there in these cases. Many more inexplicable plays/ occurrences take place off and on.

There is no dearth of people who would retort, "You say that all cricket is a puppet show, then please tell how all this happens." They must understand that I scientifically proved ten years ago what I say, beyond any ifs and buts. No one in this world full of scholars has ever been able to counter that, very long 10 years already having gone by. The world has simply maintained a haughty silence, not having had any other recourse to defend the big crime! Since then, it's all lying established even otherwise in the public domain, if logic and common-sense had any meaning for the humanity. I have brought that also out repeatedly through my books and other writings. It was for the authorities to thoroughly investigate a proven crime and to unearth the modus-operandi and bring the culprits to book. And believe me, it is not at all difficult if the authorities so desire. They have only to question some non-hardened criminals, say

some new players of the state leagues, and they will know everything in a jiffy. Remember, the modus operandi of the puppet-show has to be same, whatever be the status of a match! **If all the authorities and the rest of the world have decided to remain firmly blind, deaf, and dumb; surely that can't be any individual's fault or failure.**

How does the police solve some murders? They come to know of a murder having been committed, and they come to know of who had committed it through their investigations. They then catch hold of the murderer and make him/her explain the whole modus-operandi.

It was for this purpose, for thorough investigations in the stupendous open crime, to ascertain the modus-operandi, and of course to bring it to a halt that I knocked at the doors of the Supreme Court of India in late 2017, involving a lot of efforts and leg work; to be thoroughly disappointed by that august institution.

Yes, the reality of Cricket is too improbable to believe, yet it is crystal clear for anyone who wants to open his/her eyes and see. **It's impossible that the matches are not thoroughly scripted like a puppet show!! Exactly as the world was told again in 2020 by the insider Sanjeev Chawla.**

❐

IPL, Betting, and Fixing

Why are cricket matches or IPL matches fixed as these are? This should be one of the paramount questions in the readers' mind? Is it done to make the matches more interesting, to keep the viewers' hooked, that the one-sided stale matches are alternated with last ball nail-biting thrillers? Many of the innocent readers, not much aware of the big bad world of cricket betting and sports betting, may think so. I won't say that they would be entirely wrong, since that is one of the intended by-products; though the real and primary reason for which such a stupendous crime continues 24×7 is to continuously loot the tens of millions of addicted bettors world-wide.

To appreciate this aspect of cricket fixing, one must have an idea of the volume of the betting amounts. In my last book on the subject, '*Beat the Cricket Mafia and Win (Yes, You can do it!)*', I have estimated it to be in excess of 30 billion dollars per day! I again tried to estimate these volumes during IPL 2023. In one match on the 23rd April, 2023 (there were 2 matches that day) alone, I found the estimated volumes of betting to be in the same range. And then in one of the knock-out matches that followed, the volumes were just the double!! It is the betting volumes in IPL matches that make IPL so much sought after and, in a way, the bigger brand than Cricket itself, undoubtedly the most marketed and cherished cricket league.

Tens or hundreds of millions of people across the globe, at any point of time, remain firm addicts of cricket betting. Many

times more than them, hooked on to the game for the thrills and entertainment they get from it, are pure cricket fans, having nothing to do with the betting. They just enjoy the game, the thrills, and the atmosphere while viewing the matches in grounds or with family and friends on their TV sets. They don't give two hoots whether the matches they were viewing were natural competitive cricket or puppet shows.

The cricket fans naturally get emotionally attached to their countries. They forget everything, and just want their country to win (even though, the team they root for belongs to some Board, and is not a team having to do anything with the government of their country, e.g., India). Similarly in various leagues, they emotionally attach themselves to some team, mostly the team in the name of/representing their city or region, and just root for it in the fake matches; to rejoice when their team wins.

The above applies all the more to the Indian fans. The fact of almost empty stands in the World Cup matches of 2023 when India was not playing shows that the Indians are not that much interested in Cricket per se. They get attracted to it because of their misplaced sense of nationalism and because India does well in this sport, or to be more precise, is made to do well by the puppeteers That is done to keep the hundreds of millions of cricket crazy Indians hooked on to the game. They continue to be fooled by the aggressive marketing through the media, exploiting their sense of nationalism. More the cricket fans, more will the bettors be!

The cricket bettors get much greater thrill from betting on the matches, and mainly it is this thrill that keeps them addicted. But they pay a heavy price for their continuous addiction, getting thoroughly exploited by the cricket mafia thru ball-by-ball scripting of the matches.

Just think of the mind-boggling astronomical betting volumes! With the scope of cricket fast expanding through inclusion of more and more countries and women's cricket becoming more and more popular and prevalent, these volumes are fast increasing ever. And here we are talking of just one sport, Cricket, about thorough fixing of which we are as sure as about the existence of Sun! There are much bigger sports involving much higher volumes of betting, such as Football, and in all probability as thoroughly fixed. One thing leads to another. If humans were to become serious about fixed Cricket anytime, with the existing encyclopaedia of evidence knocking at the doors of the human world for last 10 long years, I am sure very soon the skeletons from the other cupboards will also start tumbling out.

So, when you see a hattrick of wickets or 6's in a match or batters or bowlers or fielders doing hara-kiri, it's not a result of any naturally happening phenomenon; but is the performance by the puppets to decide the fate of bets worth millions of dollars after each ball or to affect the fate of the continuing bets worth much more. So is the case with any other ball, even if no boundary is scored, or no wicket falls. Some bet or another gets decided after every ball, like runs to be scored etc. Other than on match result, and on runs to be scored in a set of overs (session betting) or in an over, many fancy bets are continuously taking place such that one or another bet gets decided or affected at the end of almost every ball.

Top batsmen failing and tailenders piling up runs in a match happens often since it will be least expected by the punters/ bettors. After a team has lost a match for all purposes quite early while chasing a target, the last one or two wickets start hitting sixes and fours at will, to make punters betting for innings score lose since no one can or would expect such an occurrence. The

odds for match result are already dead and remain dead despite flurry of sixes at that stage. The batsmen getting out for golden ducks and a flurry of sixes in an over (when match is still alive) occur since the mafia has to give a sudden twist to the odds.

The field of cricket betting is very vast like an ocean; and it has its own science with the sole aim of continuously fooling the tens or hundreds of millions of cricket bettors worldwide, with the help of the puppet shows in the grounds controlled totally by the cricket betting mafia. Everything happening in cricket grounds is inter-connected for that purpose. At the same time, the façade of natural cricket (for the ignorant masses) continues.

The matches being scripted and remote-controlled becomes too obvious at times. It amazes me how the viewers are not able to sense that!!

Also, there is no dearth of people who believe that IPL matches are fixed (probably only vaguely, and with no idea of the volumes of the money involved and the other astounding implications of the fraud), but they are too naïve to believe the same for the international matches or women's cricket. They easily forget that it is the same players and the same controlling authorities, whether league cricket or international cricket; whether men's cricket or women's cricket.

Whether you don't know or are unconcerned, doesn't matter. A very big crime and fraud is continuously taking place affecting the whole humanity alright! When you find that after a big halo is built around some players for their batting/bowling prowess, and after that when they repeatedly flop, performing well only in some odd match, though continuing to be in the playing elevens for various teams across the globe for years; it happens so for no other reason or purpose than to fool the

punters. The innocent punters expect them to perform match after match and bet accordingly. When they flop (their failures may be made to look very natural at times), the punters banking on them to perform lose repeatedly. The examples abound by hundreds, so it may not be correct to take just a few names at random. I am sure the readers themselves can think of many examples without much effort.

Similarly, when the batters suddenly and inexplicably very clearly throw away their wickets just when their team was on a winning course (sometimes historical), that is done to shock the punters and make them lose when they had become too sure of winning their bets. The example (very fresh in memory at the time of drafting this para) is Afghan batters throwing away their wickets in the Asia Cup match against Sri Lanka on the 5th September, 2023 every time their team appeared on course to win and qualify for the Super 4 stage. One may especially like to see the eighth and the ninth wickets of Najibullah Zadran and Mujeeb Ur Rahman.

When the seemingly impossible happens the other way, like Rinku Singh hitting 5 consecutive sixes of last 5 balls to win the match (no batter can do it until aided by the bowler!), same principle applies. The punters not only get trapped in such matches, but lose subsequently in many more matches expecting repeat of such feats now or then (hardly ever getting repeated😊)!

When you find that a team hitting boundaries at will with many wickets in hand suddenly collapses or just pushes and prods in the end overs, no cricket is taking place; that is done to make the millions of punters lose money in **session betting** since by then they naturally start expecting more boundaries in the end overs and a very high score (immediate example at the time of drafting this para: England batting vs New Zealand in

the 3rd ODI on the 13th September, 2023). At times, manipulation is so done that the odds don't change much for the match result such that the punters don't get any/much advantage on that front. Similarly, opposite also happens (example: just the ODI before, the 2nd ODI, between the same two teams on the 10th September, 2023); when after losing quick wickets initially, the team goes on to get a sizable score. Such occurrences are very often; the mafia does make as much money as possible at the cost of the hundreds of millions of addicted bettors. As explained in my earlier books, similar thing doesn't happen every time, since that will make the mafia lose all the edge.

The manipulation of session score is happening all the time (and that necessitates ball-by-ball scripting), in all the matches. It is done in many ways. **The purpose is always one, to fool the punter every time or almost every time. To make punter believe/expect what will happen next and then suddenly change the course.** For session of innings score, the dramatic turns take place many times in last 2-3 overs of the innings for this very reason.

In a big tournament like IPL-2023, one can come across most of such variations in various matches. One can specially have a look at match numbers 5, 9, 12, 14, 26, 27, 29, 30, 31, 32, 40, 43, 48, 53, 56, 57, 62, 63, and 66 of this tournament for the purpose. For example, in match number 5, MI went on to score 171/7 after being 48/4 in 8.5 overs and 105/6 in 15.3 overs; in match number 9, KKR went on to score 204 after being 89/5 in 11.3 overs; in the 12th match, MI could muster only 157/8 after being 64/1 in 6.3 overs; in the 62nd match, GT could manage only 188/9 after being 169/3 in 16.3 overs etc. etc.

The punters also get looted when they start expecting dramatic turn and nothing of the sort happens. Many totally

one-sided matches where one team fails to compete at all are scripted for this purpose. One finds that in various leagues, for a while such matches take place where teams make a comeback. When the punters/bettors start expecting such performances in next matches, teams start losing hopelessly😊. Caribbean Premier League, 2023 is a very good example of this.

The same team or the same player doing wonderfully well in one match and just the opposite in the very next match or vice versa is the result of same phenomenon - to make punter believe/ expect what will happen next and then stun him. Scores by the team LSG in IPL-2023 are a pertinent example of it.

Selection of most of the teams in leagues or international matches is done depending on what role is to be given to whom, injuries to the players being genuine sometimes and sometimes just declared😊. Like in movies, great heroic feats or highly villainous actions are performed by the players in regard to Cricket, acting out their roles. I know today that when I used to get so excited by Sachin Tendulkar's heroics in the ground or by the opening partnership of Sanath Jayasuriya and Romesh Kaluwitharana of Sri Lanka, or otherwise, no real Cricket was being played. To get out or hit a boundary or a six at the required moment is not much difficult (for the chosen players) with the cooperation of all others in the ground.

Timing of wickets or scoring is all governed by how the odds are to proceed/change (taking due care of session betting and other fancy bets at the same time); it has nothing to do with natural cricket. All the accompanying blabber by the commentators is only to keep the hundreds of millions of innocent viewers fooled. Keeping the masses fooled is necessary for the success and continuance of this monumental crime.

In various leagues over the globe, the most of the teams are equally strong. Also, the teams of many countries appear to be equally strong. Yet, most of the matches that take place are hopelessly one-sided. **That is because it suits the betting mafia.** If most of the matches fluctuated between the two teams, as these should when the two teams are equally strong and if natural competitive cricket is played, then the bettors/punters across the globe will get ample opportunities to be in a win-win position irrespective of the ultimate result of the match. In a match, the odds are not stationary, but are always moving with the progress of a match. The fluctuating matches are thrown in between to serve two purposes. One, it is such matches that attract more and more people to betting, and once attracted, most of them become addicted. Two, all matches can't be scripted to be one sided, since the punters/bettors have to be kept guessing all the time. Then, it is such matches that thrill and attract hundreds of millions of viewers to Cricket.

In short, all or almost all the cricket matches we view and bet upon are institutionally fixed to ensure movement of betting odds as it suits the mafia controlling cricket betting. The Cricket we view is no natural or competitive Cricket but a puppet show being performed by the players to facilitate the desired/required odds movement.

Let us think about another fundamental thing. How and on what basis the betting odds are opened and continuously changed for match result, session, or other fancy bets? Is there any mathematical/scientific formula? Answer is a big No. Who controls the odds, on what authority, and/or on what basis? It remains a matter of record that all or almost all the bookies and regular betting websites follow the same odds worldwide.

After opening arbitrarily, the odds for session and many other fancy bets may appear to be changing logically; but can there be and is there any logic for how the odds suddenly change

for match result with the progress of a match (the opening odds again being arbitrary)? When will the odds change how much, especially on fall of a wicket or on a boundary or a flurry of boundary hits? How is that decided?

There are concrete mentions in my previous books/writings of how the odds changed in matches to suit the whims of the mafia, defying logic. Those who bet and keenly follow the odds can come across this phenomenon, match after match.

If one were to apply mind to management (that mostly is manipulation) **of the odds alone, one would understand that the betting and rigging had to go together.** There is a clear record of this fact also that the odds in cricket were managed by the mafia well knowing what was going to happen in a match. That has been in full knowledge of the media and the judicial commissions appointed on the subject of fixing in cricket, since almost a decade. **But unfortunately, to ignore it has suited all.** This has amply been brought out earlier by me, also to the knowledge of the Supreme Court of India. Alas! the world has been acting blind to this hard and very valuable fact also!

Now, the above gives rise to an extremely important revelation. Management of odds doesn't apply to Cricket alone. It applies equally to other sports also, some like soccer or football, with globally many times more betting volumes, included. In football, like in Cricket, there is no formula how the odds will change when a goal gets scored. It is all arbitrary at the whims of the betting mafia.

The above is no rocket-science; it follows from very basic application of simple common-sense. Yet, the vast humanity chooses to be blind to it, to remain oblivious of this for ever!

The teams or players in the ground are never competing. On the contrary, they are always coordinating along with

the match officials to ensure that the end result of each ball is same as was ordained. The moment when a bowler will bowl that great delivery and the batsman will play the shot to get out is decided by the directors of the puppet show (exactly as Sanjeev Chawla told); the same applies to hitting of boundaries, brilliant catches, dropped catches etc. When the die-hard fans of Tendulkar or Kohli or Dhoni or Bumrah were being titillated by their hero's heroic efforts in the ground, it all was the result of the scripts written elsewhere.

In execution of the puppet shows, some aberrations may take place at times, but that won't matter much in the overall scheme as necessary corrections will take place in subsequent plays. **Here, one must understand that it is much more difficult to play-act and achieve the precise result at each ball as the script demanded, than to play natural cricket. For the former, the players we see have to be experts like robots.** They must being trained hard for the job, being trained hard for their role for a day!

Irrespective of whether anybody is betting or not, everyone has been viewing only puppet shows in the IPL and other cricket matches, by the cricketers of flesh and blood, being continuously performed for the benefit of the cricket betting mafia. **How so improbable that may appear, it will be and has been self-defeating for the human world not to wake up to the reality and all that it implies.**

Most of the cricket fans don't know much about the world of cricket betting, except that they are vaguely aware that there is some betting somewhere on a match result. And most of them consider themselves to be experts on Cricket (I also used to think so before I came to know of all about betting😊), knowing nothing about the big bad world of cricket-betting. Most (may

be almost all) of the cricket journalists and esteemed editors also are like that. It is nothing but cricket-betting that governs and controls Cricket and plays in the grounds, and not vice-versa as the masses believe or, more accurately, they have been led and conditioned to believe.

Though almost any possible question that may come to any mind (the questions will be many since Cricket is a very vast fraud) lies answered in my various writings over a very big period of 10 years, I hope the above will suffice for any intelligent reader to understand what is what as far as Cricket is concerned.

There is a big world of cricket betting since there are tens of millions of cricket bettors world-wide. Some of them are aware of fixing to varying extents, while a larger number are innocent and ignorant. They all are too bothered about own win or loss in betting to bother much about fixing and its far-reaching implications or consequences. I say this as a result of my interactions with some of them over the years.

Needless to say, given what Cricket really is, **the books (other than on technical aspects of the game) on it (with the underlying assumption that it was a competitive sport), tonnes of pages of newspapers and magazines written for decades on scores of aspects of the game, the discussions and all the blabber on various sports and news channels on those various aspects for years and years etc., has all been total trash and bunkum,** coming from the highly respected hundreds and thousands of people! Because for past some decades at least, real Cricket was hardly ever being played.

We have been living in such a ridiculous world!!

❒

A Crime Most Extraordinary

During IPL-2023, on an average an open fraud worth more than 30 billion dollars was taking place daily. It was a most extraordinary crime in more than one way. Let us try to look at some of these aspects.

1. Mostly the crimes are committed surreptitiously, away from the public eye. This was a crime committed in broad day light, in full view of thousands of people in the grounds, and tens of millions viewing it live on various screens outside the grounds.

2. In a crime, there are criminals and there are victims. This was a crime, cherished, supported and celebrated most by the victims – the tens and hundreds of millions of the cricket fans and the cricket bettors alike. Most of the victims are either unaware of the crime till date or feel totally unconcerned.

3. This is a publicly proven crime that puts all the mighty including the PM of India, the whole Indian political dispensation, the biggest corporate leaders, the Supreme Court of India, the law-enforcing agencies of India, ICC, BCCI, the Indian and the global Media etc., in the dock. The book *'We the Oodles'* and some other books and writings stand testimony for ever to this irrefutable fact.

4. It is a crime publicly exposed and proven; yet it continues unhindered and unchallenged. Not only that, it is prospering by leaps and bounds. Does it happen so with any other crime?

5. One does come across the billions of human beings feeling worried about this or that petty or big fraud or crime, proven or suspected; yet no one or hardly anyone was/is worried about this giant crime, lying well proved in the public domain. This also makes it most extraordinary.

6. It is the humans who talk and deliberate a lot about morality, and right or wrong. When the same humans coolly accept and celebrate such an open and mega crime as IPL-2023, all their collective morality dies a natural death. **In fact, all their endeavours, political or otherwise, get dwarfed, except probably some scientific accomplishments.** Because we are talking here of a global crime, that was continuously marketed day and night by the media itself and vastly affects today's human world, though the world remains largely unaware of the deep implications; and the crime continues to prosper still.

7. It was a crime where the executing criminals i.e., the cricketers, were and are treated as demi-gods by the large public around the world, and projected so by the Media.

8. When the crime was taking place openly, there was a team of commentators, ex-cricketers, and cricket journalists and experts to fool the world, continuously working hard to camouflage the crime so that the people don't become aware of it. It worked openly and in full public view as the accomplices.

9. It was one of the most/best marketed events or extravaganzas. That makes it an extraordinarily marketed crime as well.

10. We generally find media making a lot of noise against public frauds and crimes. Here was a crime not only kept hidden by the media from the public, but also promoted the most by it, whether print or electronic media.

11. Last, but not the least, the financial value of the fraud, estimated to be in excess of 30 billion dollars daily, makes it the most extra-ordinary crime.

One probably may list many more such extraordinary aspects of the colossal public crime known as IPL-2023. But the above list gives the reader an essence of how IPL-2023 and Cricket have been a most extraordinary crime. We shall see some of the above in a bit more detail in the subsequent chapters.

❐

When All Law-Enforcers became Non-Existent

Humans have made laws and they nurture a big and much detailed system for law enforcement. After becoming sure of how cricket was a big public crime, I exposed it publicly about 10 years ago. That alone should have made the various law-enforcing agencies of the country and the world act. There is no reason why ICC and its anti-corruption unit (ACU) should have not come into full swing. But to my shock and utter surprise, not a finger moved anywhere. That was despite I personally knocked at the doors of the ACU of ICC repeatedly.

So, I went ahead and directly contacted the various authorities and the political leaders of India as well, years ago. That is all documented in my book 'Cricket the Massive Fraud', but still never a finger moved anywhere. I also wrote to the then Home Minister Rajnath Singh and Mr Ajit Doval, the National Security Advisor, drawing their personal attention to the ongoing massive fraud through Cricket. The vast implications, like terror funding, do fall within the area of work of Mr Doval also. Absolutely no result, again.

I reproduce below my last letter sent to CBI (also mentioned on my facebook page https://www.facebook.com/atulrailway/posts/pfbid02zk2w8fCMHXWMeXdtgK4qKhvsQdtFKau-d7zAQQwqjLhrj4w5MsQNsSA2brsYgAsG7l):

"Dated: 16/05/2022

The Director,
Central Bureau of Investigation
Plot No. 5-B
6th Floor
CGO Complex
Lodhi Road
New Delhi - 110003

Subject: Cricket betting and match-fixing

Dear Sir,

I tried to communicate to the CBI through its website using the facility 'Submit a Tip', but couldn't succeed since the facility was mal-functioning in all probability. Hence this letter.

This is in reference to a recent news item with the headline: 'CBI to probe pan-India IPL betting network with links to Pakistan'. The malice is much larger and deeper than comes out in this news, or what CBI appears to know.

To know better, if not already known to you, please go through the attached text and a recent news item in the Statesman (clipping attached for your kind ready perusal). These should make CBI understand what is what, if it so wishes, and if it is not already aware.

I shall request CBI to please investigate the whole thing meaningfully and act as early as possible such that 50 billion dollars a day continuous open public fraud comes to an end. It is for these amounts going from the pockets of innocent bettors that the whole drama of IPL and cricket in general is taking place round the clock through institutionally fixed cricket. What is mentioned in the news item is probably not even the tip of the iceberg.

CBI must be knowing better why it has not been acting on an exposed and open public fraud for last 10 years. Out of its own complicity, or out of some other compulsions? Since everything has so much been in the public domain that probably CBI can't feign ignorance.

I have also urged CBI directly to act at times earlier, if my memory serves me right.

In case of any doubt, CBI may please feel free to contact me. Thank you.

(ATUL KUMAR)
phone no. and Email id"

As expected, the much-coveted Central Bureau of Investigation of India, became as non-existent as it has always been on this matter and other matters of great public import. Not only that, I never heard again as to what became of the probe, the CBI was to undertake.

Then there are other law-enforcing agencies, a number of those in India, starting from the police. The police were very active during the Sreesanth episode. Then also they ignored the obvious and aided by the rogue media, kept the public in the dark. That was detailed in the chapter, *'Large Scale Fixing Gets Established but All look the Other Way'* in the book 'Bettors Beware' published as long back as 2013. The ex-police commissioners (the one who was in the chair at the time of the Sreesanth episode) have written books on the subject of the shady world of cricket. But they have shown their utter ignorance, if not idiocy, and have totally misguided the readers, as has been the case with various films etc.

Here I must mention of a top news heading in the Asian Age of the 18th May, 2013. That was soon after the Sreesanth episode.

The heading said, **'IPL rot deeper, but no hard evidence: Cops.'** If the cops knew that the rot was deeper, who stopped them from getting/unearthing the evidence. One has to toil to get the evidence. No?

But in this case, an encyclopaedia of evidence, including the scientific evidence, is available on a platter, for a decade now, for anyone to use it and act. C**learly enough, everyone, whether belonging to the authorities or to the media, is interested only in idle and hollow talks, as most of those around us are!**

Today, not only crime is taking place openly, the authorities choosing to keep a dark black cloth wrapped around their closed eyes; but it is also being marketed as such by the hundreds of tipsters active on the social media. They openly say match after match that they have got report on the fixed match as to which team would win and how many runs will be scored or not scored in how many overs. **They do their own bit openly as agents of the mafia to trap the innocent bettors/punters.** (It is detailed in my last book: 'Beat the Cricket Mafia and Win (Yes, you can do it)'). No authority, either from the cricket world or otherwise ever bothers to find out what was happening! They all feel happy doing nothing, continuing with their meaningless existence! **The open crime merrily goes on prospering!!**

Let us not forget how powerful these agencies are! They can and do raid even very powerful ministers and political leaders. They can take anyone to task anytime, rightfully or otherwise. Their true character as evident from the above does make one wonder how well would they be carrying their day-to-day responsibilities!

❒

Judiciary in the Dock

The humans have evolved a very detailed system of governing themselves over thousands of years. Probably judiciary has place at the top in our governance. All of us are liable to go to the dock in a court of law for any wrong doing. **But what becomes of our evolution and existence when the judiciary puts itself in the dock? And that too in a very big way?**

After great difficulty, I went to the Supreme Court of India, the highest judicial authority in my country, India, in end 2017 and was successful in filing a detailed writ petition (1163/2017) telling the court how Cricket was totally scripted and institutionally fixed (successful submission of the petition was far from easy). Since all the other authorities had failed to act for years despite repeated requests, I requested the Hon'ble Court to act suitably to bring the ongoing massive fraud to a halt and to get it thoroughly investigated to ascertain the modus-operandi. Honestly, I had very high hopes from the revered institution, though some people very close to me (including my mother) told me that nothing would come out of my efforts. **Unfortunately, they proved right.**

It is a big story and is chronicled in my book 'We the Oodles.' A copy of this book was religiously sent by me to the Supreme Court of India as well, among other constitutional authorities and some big names in the media. Nothing happened even after that.

Though the Supreme Court of India was smart enough (probably wrong to say 'smart' since this institution has unquestionable authority) to be successful in sweeping the matter under the carpet eventually, not being able to dismiss it somehow; in the process it did expose itself. Now through my laboured book '*We the Oodles*' now it stands in the dock for ever (or till it rectifies its sins, possibility of the same looking very remote). I am sure that the discerning readers would realise that I couldn't be saying what I have said above, if I was not standing on an absolutely strong footing. My position vis-à-vis the all powerful and mighty Supreme Court of India becomes invincible since the august institution has failed to act for years even after my book, *We the Oodles*. In fact, all the authorities of India, and of course of BCCI and ICC, are in the dock for ever, having no defence, for inaction for years and years despite all my efforts through books and otherwise.

One more development that took place as a result of the WP (C) 1163/2017 in the Supreme Court of India was that the COA (Committee of Administrators) of BCCI headed by Mr Vinod Rai had a meeting with me (along with my co-petitioner) in July 2018 along with their full team. The details of that meeting including the crass cheating by the COA (and Mr Vinod Rai) later on are also chronicled in the book *We the Oodles*. Had the COA stood even by the small promise (of investigating the final of IPL 10) made during the meeting, probably some chain of corrections would have set in. But of course, that could never suit the all-powerful mafia! Anyway, the real face of a person of the stature of Mr Vinod Rai also got exposed!!

I urge the readers to please try to understand the gravity of the above for 1300 million plus Indians and the world (Cricket being a very big international crime). The Supreme Court of India is the watchdog for the Constitution of India and almost

the supreme authority in the country whose decisions can make governments fall. Hardly a day goes when the Supreme Court doesn't appear in one or another news heading. It has very vast reach and power, deciding on most of the matters concerning public, including very contentious religious issues. For example, please have a look at these news headings: '*SC: File cases against all making hate speeches*' (Statesman of 29/4/2023) and '*Govts have no right to stay in office if they let people die: SC*' (TOI of 7/11/2019).

It was to such an august and powerful institution that I and my co-petitioner, two credible citizens of the country, went for curbing a mammoth public fraud and crime. I had high hopes since our petition listed and explained too much indisputable evidence of the crime. What did the revered Supreme Court of India do? Effectively nothing! What is the result? A public fraud worth more than 30 or 50 billion dollars daily has been continuing ever since. **That would mean a further loot out of conservatively estimated betting amounts of 5 × 365 × 30 = 54,750 or let us say 50000 billion dollars or 50 trillion dollars (or thereabouts) has already taken place just because of inaction by the Supreme Court of India.** That amount is equivalent to approximately 4000 crore crore of rupees or 4000000000 crores of rupees. **And the mind-boggling daily fraud still continues, ever increasing, much in excess of 10 trillion dollars per year!**

Just imagine, what would happen if these sums were not to go to the pockets of a few (thousands of people, given the vastness of the fraud and the crime), and were to remain in the pockets of the masses and in the public system! And imagine combining much more loot through soccer and other sports! How much all of us would stand to gain, if the loot is curbed!!

And imagine the enormity of the sin of the authorities, the governments, and the much-revered Supreme Court of India by acting deaf and blind to let such a massive fraud continue!!!

Apart from the above mind-boggling financial implications, the failure of the Supreme Court to act has huge implications for overall governance. That would mean that a citizen of India has nowhere to go for necessary corrections required in the public interest, for redressal of very genuine grievances. That means the total loss of credibility of the supreme institution of a vast country, **thereby meaning anarchy.** That means that the very spirit of the Constitution of India stands abused by the institution that is supposed to be its watchdog!!

If the credibility of the Supreme Court of India remains so shattered; what about the credibility of the other judicial authorities, in fact, of the whole judicial system in India?

With the fact of the unimaginable open massive public fraud continuing unhindered even after public exposure in 2013, the law, law-enforcers, legal systems, and legal processes etc. have all been lying truly dead and buried in India. With the fraud becoming very open of late, the anarchy has almost been complete.

❐

The Criminal Media

When everyone else fails a citizen, he/she looks up to the Media. This is how it has been. But when one comes to know and understands that media was the greater culprit than the others, what does one do?

Let us have a look at some of the newspaper headlines about IPL matches during IPL-2023, or just afterwards. The name of the newspaper and date of the match/report are indicated alongside within the brackets.

No end to Delhi's woes', (TOI (Times of India) 11/4/2023, DC vs MI)

Royals survive late Dhoni blitz (TOI, 12/4/2023)

Green gives SRH the Blues (TOI, 18/4/2023)

Walk in the Park for CSK (TOI, 21/4/2023)

Take responsibility for the loss Rana (Statesman, 21/4/2023, DC vs KKR)

Superkings slay Knights (TOI, 23/4/2023)

Jaiswal Spinners take RR to the top (TOI, 27/4/2023)

Wishes pour in for Rohit Sharma as he turns 36 (Statesman, 30/4/2023)

Bowlers win it for Capitals (TOI, 24/4/2023, DC vs SRH)

Super Giants Super Show (TOI, 28/4/2023 LSG vs PBKS)

Ishant & Co. deliver win against all odds (TOI, 2/5/2023, DC vs GT)

SKY Rockets MI to Third (TOI, 9/5/2023, RCB vs MI)

KKR prevail in death-overs battle (TOI, 4/5/2023, KKR vs RR)

Pooran Blinder takes LSG over the line (TOI, 13/5/2023, LSG vs SRH)

RCB's dominant bowling display rout RR by 112 runs (Statesman, 14/5/2023)

Titans first to qualify; sun sets on Sunrisers (TOI, 15/5/2023)

KKR's moment of truth (TOI, for ensuing KKR vs LSG match on 20/5/2023)

MI beat LSG, sensational 5/5 by Akash Madhwal (Statesman, 24/5/2023)

Titans hope to gatecrash MSD party (TOI, 28/5/2023)

Shubman got amazing ability and temperament to perform (Statesman, 7/6/2023)

These are only some of the headlines in some of the newspapers. During IPL, almost all newspapers (at least of India, if not of most of the other cricket playing countries) carried big reports on the match/matches the previous day, many newspapers carrying more than one report daily. These all reports indicated as if competitive matches were taking place, as if natural cricket was being played. The whole media, including the electronic media, continued with such reports; even though it had been brought to its knowledge 10 years ago that all such cricket

matches were fixed. There is even a PTI report to that effect on record. **By wilfully hiding a big public crime, and projecting a proven mammoth fraud and crime as some competitive sport, the Indian and the global media did indulge in a very big criminal act, by facilitating and marketing the fraud.** None in the media has any defence, whether the Statesman or any other newspaper or TV channel that kept on reporting about IPL matches as competitive sport. The media can't feign that it didn't know the reality.

The report titled 'Snakes, Ladders and last-over thrills' by Pulakesh Mukhopadhyay (Statesman on upcoming match between RR and KKR on 11/5/2023) had this interesting mention: '*And, of course, last-over heroics always mean television's unalloyed delight over the ads seen for so many hours across the land and beyond*'; even though it indicated just some partial truth.😊

The commentary, the panel discussions, various analyses, utterances by cricketers and ex-cricketers (like https://www.espncricinfo.com/story/hardik-pandya-on-gujarat-titans-loss-we-lost-because-i-could-not-get-my-rhythm-1372888, https://www.espncricinfo.com/story/ipl-punjab-vs-dc-warner-says-delhi-batters-have-found-it-challenging-at-home-1376587, https://www.hindustantimes.com/cricket/i-couldn-t-sleep-sochta-raha-kya-alag-mohit-sharma-opens-up-on-heartbreaking-last-over-vs-csk-101685470293194.html, and https://www.insidesport.in/ipl-2023-anil-kumble-hails-impact-player-rule-says-lot-of-200-plus-scores-this-season-due-to-impact-player-rule/); the experts' views about players/matches in print as well as the electronic media etc., all are brought to us by the media. When we consider what is the reality of all these matches and the players that were talked about, we should be able to clearly see what non-

sense and falsity we are bombarded with, day and night, by the criminal and rogue media. Here my short facebook post https://www.facebook.com/atulrailway/posts/pfbid036eL5bzEP5eCF3YopzY8fhsLP4jWG7LSbA46ingF2RweDwJZHbLeSPqPDk1TziJJ4l of 22nd April, 2023 becomes relevant. It is reproduced here:

'When the sports pages of all newspapers across the globe, none excluded, are full of nothing but falsehood and trash, how can and why should anyone believe about anything else said in those very newspapers? Same applies to any other medium.'

The much reputed English daily 'the Statesman' (I personally consider it the most reputed because of its integrity) is a very good example of one hand not knowing what the other hand is doing. Even such a reputed newspaper exemplifies the inherent contradictions in human behaviour, and the resulting senseless human existence. In this very newspaper, there was an editorial 'IPL imploding' (Statesman of 20/5/2012), and another editorial 'Scrap the COA' (Statesman of 13/12/2018). COA meant Committee of Administrators of the BCCI (Board of Control for Cricket in India). There have been many other write-ups over the years in this paper by its sports editor, Mr Pulakesh Mukhopadhyay, some of those mentioning me or quoting me, telling as to how cricket was all corrupted for the benefit of the betting industry. The news report 'Cricket in Massive Fix?' quoting me (Statesman of 10/7/2013) and a very positive review of my book 'Bettors Beware' (titled 'Bookmaker's Paradise, bettor's doom', Statesman of 27/4/2014) were published in this very newspaper. With all this knowledge of thorough corruption in Cricket, the Statesman has daily been publishing big news reports on the cricket matches still, as if competitive cricket had been taking place!! It did so with the matches of IPL-2023 also.😊

I don't know if its esteemed editor understands what disservice even the Statesman had been doing to the humanity by its daily reports conveying that competitive cricket was being played in the matches reported upon. ☹ I am sure he must be quite satisfied in his knowledge that he was following some principles of journalism he had been taught, not much worried about the end result of his actions, and not having any guilty conscience. Same would apply to most of the other esteemed editors.

While I say above, I must mention that personally I shall remain indebted to the Statesman and its editor for ever for not only acknowledging my efforts earlier, but also for bringing those out to the world. It was Statesman only that published my interview under the heading '***Bureaucrats are both running and ruining the country***', just below its mast head, as the main news report, on 12/8/2010, in the aftermath of my efforts about procurement through cartels in the Indian Railways. That was a very rare honour, the most valuable to me till date. It has been the Statesman only that has been telling the public about corruption in Cricket, quoting me also, now and then, for last many years.

Let us now see a recent write-up of May, 2023. '**Generally, a bad ball is just a bad ball; no one plays to lose**' by the veteran sports journalist **Mr Suresh Menon** (https://www.thehindu.com/sport/cricket/generally-a-bad-ball-is-just-a-bad-ball-no-one-plays-to-lose/article66831061.ece#:~:text=Premium,-May%20 10%2C%202023). The write-up starts like this:

'It is now a fact of life that when a player has a bad day on the field at the IPL, he will be trolled by his team's fans, by neutrals, and anybody with a social media account. The latest to receive the full blast of public opprobrium is Rajasthan Royals' Sandeep Sharma who bowled a no-ball and conceded a last-ball six to allow Sunrisers Hyderabad to squeak through.

No one plays to lose (we won't get into the seamier side of sport here, although some of the trolls raised it),....'

It pains and shocks to see how ignorant even such senior journalists are. Or are they ignorant because it suits their very existence to be ignorant? They would lose all their relevance if the world came to know of what Cricket and sports in general have been? They will look big fools in the mirror for ignorantly having told the public about Cricket and sports all their life as these never were? If people like Mr Suresh Menon were to know today, if they already don't know (that looks more likely in this case), what the reality of Cricket was and what all was already in the public domain related to that, they would feel highly ashamed of their professional existence provided they had any self-respect!

Also as mentioned earlier, it is a classic example of how most of the deemed experts of sports have no knowledge at all of betting in sports and of how the sports are governed by betting. Yes, it's not supposed that anyone plays to lose; but precisely that happens, because the players are not playing, they are only carrying the dictates of the betting mafia. **Ignorance of hundreds or thousands of veteran journalists can't and doesn't change the reality.**

Ignorance can't and doesn't absolve the journalists of their sins either. **They all have been sinning whenever they gave a message to the public through their professional actions that cricket being played was competitive.** Especially, during last 10 years. Those who have been doing so despite knowing the reality, or wilfully ignoring the reality, have been committing a criminal act.

I know that I am sounding very harsh, but it should be understood that daily loot in excess of 30 billion dollars is no

joke, to which all of them have been contributing, knowingly or unknowingly, actively or passively.

The following advertisements ran in Khan Market, New Delhi, for about a fortnight in December, 2022; unquestioned and unchallenged.

And yet the world of media continues to feign total ignorance of the reality. What to say?

There is another very interesting thing. There are many other aspects related to Cricket or any other sport. Media talks a lot about all those. And then the social media takes cue from it. Like ball tempering, IPL auctions, team selections, changing rules etc. But they all keep quiet on the subject of institutionalized fixing in IPL or Cricket, something so big that in the face of it most of the other aspects so vigorously talked about die a natural death. Probably that has to do more with the general human stupidity, we shall see a little later.

The above brings out the true character not only of the Indian Media, but also of the global media. And it is this media, the news and discussions brought to us through it, that control and govern our thinking, our very consciousness, whether we realise or not. Even though many of us remain vaguely aware of the loss of credibility of the present-day media, yet the social media starts buzzing with whatever the media takes up. And the contrary is even more true. There is no issue if it's not an issue as per the Media, like daily loot of 30 billion dollars through cricket and much greater corruption in the sports as a whole!

At least in India, we find media suddenly taking up/ raking up issues of public frauds, systemic or by individuals, with utmost fervour, and as suddenly forgetting everything even though nothing had reached logical conclusion even remotely. Examples abound. Big loss of public money through procurement through cartels in the Indian Railways, Lalit Modi, Robert Vadra, Vijay Mallya etc. What it does is to just create narratives from time to time to keep itself occupied while controlling the public consciousness for ulterior motives (many times its motive is to keep the public engaged in something or some non-issues to

divert its attention from the real issues). As said, it hardly ever takes things to logical conclusion for the larger good. It exists for self-service alone.

The criminality of the Media doesn't start and end with Cricket or sports. It goes much beyond.

This is what even Yuval Noah Harari said about the media in 2018: (https://timesofindia.indiatimes.com/home/sunday-times/all-that-matters/in-the-news-market-youre-not-the-customer-but-the-product-yuval-noah-harari/articleshow/65639339.cms)

"........ The struggle to capture people's attention has resulted in a destructive model for the news industry: "exciting news that costs you nothing – in exchange for your attention". Our attention is captured by sensational headlines and then sold to advertisers and politicians. In this battle for attention, there is little incentive to safeguard the truth.

You may think that you are nevertheless getting a good bargain here. You don't have to pay anything, and you are entertained with interesting stories. But, in fact you are not the customer at all, you are the product. You are being sold. You are giving up your most valuable asset – your attention – and you allow powerful corporations and politicians to brainwash you. That's crazy........."

The above expresses a lot and means a lot. Probably only Mr Harari could have told the world such a massive and harsh truth in so few precise words! Yes, that's crazy; and it's crazier that even today, after five years, same craziness continues, **even all the egoist intellectuals (or almost all) of the world happily allowing themselves to be sold by the rogue media.**

The above expression by Mr Harari also clearly brings out that the media acts as agent of the powerful corporations and politicians. If he had known about the reality of Cricket, he would, in all probability, have added the mafia to it. He also would have known that the powerful corporations and politicians are subservient to a powerful mafia or they themselves form that powerful mafia.

❒

PM Modi, Politics, and Mount Everest of Corruption

India has been having a Prime Minister (PM) since 2014 who came to power with a promise of weeding out corruption. He has been leaving no opportunity to publicly boast of zero tolerance of his government against corruption. Even very recently, in 2023, he has attacked corruption in no uncertain terms, both at national and international platforms. Corruption was one of the main themes of his Independence Day speech in 2023. One may refer https://www.indiatoday.in/india/story/pm-modi-independence-day-speech-three-evils-corruption-nepotism-appeasement-2421273-2023-08-15, and https://www.youtube.com/watch?v=TQydS0NVqXY.

For his posture on corruption at the international platform, one may refer https://www.thehindu.com/news/national/at-g20-meet-pm-modi-calls-for-collective-efforts-to-fight-corruption/article67186955.ece. Please see the following excerpts from it:

'Prime Minister Narendra Modi on Saturday, August 12, 2023, said the impact of corruption is felt most by the poor and the marginalised people. He said corruption affects the allocation of resources, markets and diminishes the people's quality of life. Addressing virtually the G-20 anti-corruption Ministerial meeting at Kolkata, the Prime Minister said, "India has a strict policy of zero tolerance against corruption." He said Nobel laureate Rabindranath Tagore had cautioned us against greed as it prevents us from realising the truth...'

What does one say when the same PM is known to have been acting totally deaf and blind to a monumental matter of corruption that was brought to his personal notice many years ago through a detailed book (the receipt duly acknowledged by his office), and about which he has been reminded periodically through letters since then. Having been so vocal against corruption, and being the chief executive of the country, it was imperative for him and was very much within his powers to order all the agencies under him to thoroughly investigate the ongoing fraud through Cricket (I was always there to help and guide any well-meaning forces), and to bring it to a halt. But he did nothing of the sort, not moving even a finger. He has absolutely no defence. **His only saviour is that there is no one to ask him any question ever on this, neither from the opposition, nor from the media.**

What is corruption? Is corruption only that what PM Modi or any Tom, Dick, or Harry thinks it to be? Or should it be decided objectively as to what is corruption? We all agree that matters of frauds, misappropriation, bribery, embezzlement, economic offences etc. are 'corruption.' Cricket and IPL have been epitomes of corruption in more ways than one.

None other than, ex ace cricketer and Indian Captain, Bishan Singh Bedi publicly said this in November 2018, *"I don't want to say anything about IPL. There's not a bigger scam in India than IPL. Nobody here knows where IPL's money comes and goes. The second edition of the IPL happened in South Africa, millions of money was taken out of the country without the permission of Finance Minister." He further went on to say, "IPL should not be the basis of Indian selection, local T20 tournaments should be. A team has players who are paid high and ones who get less money. The lower income player doesn't have the skills, how does he catch up? The only way he sees is betting. I have a lot of experience in cricket, you can tell what is happening in what*

match. If we stay blind even while seeing, then it's our choice." (https://www.indiatoday.in/sports/cricket/story/bishan-singh-bedi-indian-premier-league-1391500-2018-11-19)

Mr Bedi either doesn't know or comprehend the complete truth about Cricket, or he was not telling the complete truth about it (himself having been a cricketer). But he did talk about big misappropriation through IPL and also fixing in it in no uncertain words. **Why did no one act on it or react to it? Why was there no follow up action on such a big concern by a man of the stature of Mr Bishan Singh Bedi? What has the 'zero tolerance against corruption' government been doing for last five years?**

Is institutional fixing of IPL (an Indian affair) matches to enable betting mafia to loot tens of billions of dollars daily from the millions of cricket bettors not a matter of corruption PM Modi should have been worrying about? Given the amounts involved, the culprits involved, given how hundreds of millions of cricket fans are cheated, how openly the fraud is committed etc., does not IPL-2023 easily qualify as Mount Everest of corruption?

And when Indian PM makes public statements on corruption as brought out above, but blesses such a corruption like IPL-2023 himself by turning his back to it; **he declares himself a totally false man deserving no respect**, whatever and howsoever great be his many other achievements.

The buck doesn't stop at PM Modi and his government alone. We have a world in which political opposition crosses swords with the government in power, and media crosses swords with the politicians, on many issues. **That invariably happens in various matters of corruption or perceived corruption.** But they all combine, no one crossing any sword, when it comes to monumental corruption through IPL, Cricket, and sports in general. The corruption continues to prosper unhindered.

The above fact should suffice to tell us the reality of politics and of the world at large. That must make us clearly see and understand that all the politicians are one when it comes to real corruption. Please do reflect on that Mr Jay Shah, son of Mr Amit Shah, the Home Minister of India, is the secretary of BCCI, one of the main culprits for the corruption of IPL-2023. The opposition is always targeting Mr Amit Shah, but on this issue where his own son is totally defenceless, the opposition doesn't say a word.

When we see the politicians throwing mud at each other continuously, it's nothing but their posturing to keep the masses fooled. Like big idiots, we continue to fight with each other and even kill each other at times for our political affiliations, remaining oblivious of the fact that all the politicians equally support or feel equally unconcerned about the Mount Everest of corruption and other matters of big systemic corruption. We shed our blood for big hypocrites and self-servers.

Though that is the harsh reality of the politicians, people continue to indulge praising one political party while denouncing others. They enter into lot of hot discussions on many petty political issues, even on issues of no consequence to the humanity at large. Most of the times they are being shepherded by the Media in choosing the subject of the day for discussions. That probably applies more to the intellectual class. In short, the people spend their life time in utter ignorance.

Also, please never lose sight that not only Indian politicians, but many first world countries (and their leaders) have also to be part and parcel of this monumental corruption through Cricket.

All the politicians of India kept quiet, doing nothing, more than a decade ago also when loss to public exchequer of India to the tune of Rs 5000 crore per annum (though nothing compared to loot through IPL, yet a sizable amount) through procurement

from the cartels in the Indian Railways became public (in India, the party in opposition now was in power and the party in power now was in opposition then). The issue was brought to the personal knowledge of many leading Indian politicians by me through letters that time also. Their continuous inaction has helped continuance of the menace/evil even today.

Some questions to Arvind Kejriwal, Mamata Banerjee, Nitish Kumar, M K Stalin, Amit Shah, Yogi Adityanath, Narendra Modi, Siddaramaiah, Rahul Gandhi et al are: "You all make big public claims from time to time about fighting various public evils. That's fine (if claims are true). **You project yourselves as heroes. But when it comes to much greater evils - one of those mind-boggling and mother of many other evils, publicly known for last 10 years - why do you all become totally deaf, dumb, and blind? What are your compulsions? To which mafia are all of you subservient? Or are all of you the mafia, hand-in-glove in the biggest known crime?** That too, when the proceeds from this biggest known loot are well known to fund terrorist activities also; and you all leave no opportunity to condemn terrorism? **Is your hypocrisy unfathomable? Are you all not villains, in reality?"** There may be many more such questions.

All the politicians and the public crib, complain, and talk a lot throughout their limited lives on petty or not-so-petty matters of corruption or injustice they face or come to know of. **But by keeping quiet on or continuing to be blind to the Mount Everest of crime and corruption at the same time, for years and years, they confirm each and every word said in this book about the human world.**

❐

The Mob mentality Rules

The unhindered continuance and prosperity of the biggest publicly exposed and proven crime till date like IPL-2023 (IPL is just a subset of Cricket) confirms one thing. That it is not right or wrong, the righteousness or religion, or anything else, but the mob mentality that rules and governs the human beings. Whether uneducated or the educated, whether masses or the highly intellectual ones, all are ruled by mob mentality. It is nothing but the prevalence of mob mentality that makes things without substance highly popular and things with substance remaining unheard of. That doesn't mean that things of substance never become popular.😊

It is nothing else but mob mentality that gives rise to big fan-clubs of self-serving criminals and celebrities. It is mob mentality that makes many worthless posts viral on the social media, not many bothering about much meaningful posts. Houseful of mediocre movies, or such books becoming best seller etc. – it is all result of the mob mentality that prevails. Knowingly or unknowingly, we are continuously ruled by mob mentality, not by any objective zero-based thinking.

In the context of this book, I must make some real-life narrations. This is not done with any ill-will against anyone or with any ulterior motives, but to bring home the points objectively.

These are the times when Whatsapp groups abound. I am also a member of some groups. One of such groups is of the retired officers of Indian Railways Stores Service, the service to which I also belonged. The group consists of 100 plus members, all or almost all of whom have retired from posts at Joint Secretary to Govt of India or above level. Most of them have retired at the level of additional Secretary, and quite a few even at the level of Secretary to Govt of India. So, this group can very well be considered to be representing the cream of the Indian society, all being also the senior citizens.

Since I joined this group a few years ago, all or almost all the members of the group have been aware of the reality of cricket and my efforts on this subject, through me. In my naivete, I expected that these very responsible men of the world would act and react after they came to know of the crime and corruption that was continuing through cricket; they or at least some of them would do at least something or make some efforts to highlight/ control this scourge of the society. But nothing of the sort ever happened, despite my repeated posts in the group on the subject. At last, I posted the following in this group in the middle of May, 2023.

"I say the following with due respect to all the members of the group. There is nothing personal in it, only expression of my honest thoughts as a normal human-being. I shall request the esteemed members to receive the same with an open, free, and unbiased mind. 🙏

I am a member of this group for more than 3 years probably. Probably, not much after my joining the group, I brought out the subject of cricket being all scripted and the fact of my having filed a PIL in the Hon'ble Supreme Court of India in this respect. I might also have mentioned about books written by me on the

subject. This I am talking about my early days in the group. I doubt if initially many took me seriously, but I do hope that from what all has been coming out since then in the public domain, many if not most of the members, at least realise that I was not much wrong; though I have no idea how many still comprehend fully as to what is what and the resulting implications.

There were some brilliant (I don't mean it sarcastically) members who explicitly maintained that what I said could not be true. As usual with the rest of the world, they had their conclusions without having gone through at all as to on what basis one had been saying what. Many times, our beliefs, sometimes much hardened, don't let us listen to reason at all. It happens all the time with the human mind. In this case, to the chagrin of the perpetrators, the fraud lies even scientifically proved beyond any ifs and buts, for a decade now. It has been a big boon, in fact something like a miracle, that today I stand fully vindicated by other exposures and by none other than Time itself. In fact, everything is so open today that only those with tightly shut eyes can say that they don't know anything! 😟

I was greatly disappointed by the Supreme Court of India. I could never understand how could such an august institution openly act as a protector of the elephantine and to-date the biggest ever exposed fraud in the world and allow it not only to continue but also to prosper. And losing all its credibility in the bargain! Everything about sins of the Supreme Court of India today lies indisputably documented in the books 'We the Oodles' and 'What is killing us... Covid or Stupidity?' Today, one can also refer to the website thecricketmafia.com. This website is in existence for some months now, and was also brought to the knowledge of the world through big displays in Khan Market, New Delhi in December, 2022. The whole cricket world and all the cricketers and the authorities and others connected with the

cricket world lie openly and publicly implicated, all accepting their guilt by keeping quiet. But the mind-boggling fraud still continues to prosper!! The Supreme Court of India continues to be a big culprit!!

This group also has disappointed me no end. And this post is about that. Let us see who all are members of this group. This group has been consisting of about 100 very senior retired bureaucrats, of the level of joint secretary and above in the Govt. of India. Most of them retired above level of joint secretary. And for years now, they have constantly been made aware of the mega public fraud, its continuation, and it's too vast and serious implications, through me. And yet, while they (or some in the group) have been bothering a lot almost about every other wrong-doing, some with very petty implications in comparison, that comes to their notice; none appears to be sufficiently or at all bothered about this exposed all-encompassing fraud continuing thru cricket.

If this group was only for niceties and jokes, I would have had no business to write this post. But all sorts of national. International, and historical matters get commented upon and discussed in this group. And every one or almost everyone has strangely been maintaining a silence on this all-encompassing fraud we get bombarded with 24×7 through big newspaper and TV headlines and discussions! Why? Just because a fraud is being perpetrated by the media and the authorities themselves, it's not a fraud, howsoever big it may be, and howsoever far-reaching implications it may be having? And anything, howsoever petty or useless or meaningless should get all our attention, just because media is highlighting it? To me, it becomes even more painful when I find people much more intelligent and capable than me, having achieved much higher status than me in public life, behaving as if not at all bothered about a mega fraud but

much bothered about petty wrong-doings. How do they allow their minds to become totally subservient to the rogue media!! I do wonder if this was the infinite human stupidity Einstein talked of! Did that stupidity emanate from the lack of or non-existence of sense of proportion and common-sense in the human beings? Or did it result because all of us are governed by self-interest and need for self-preservation alone?

Many of us would say, in fact some have already said so, that what could they do or that they could do nothing. Such a reaction fills me with anger along with the sense of helplessness and total disappointment. It is not that they can't do anything, but it is because they don't want to go out of their comfort zones and don't want to do anything. There is a lot they can do even while remaining within their comfort zone. Couldn't tens of members of this group comfortably make thousands in the world aware of what is what over past few years if they had so wanted? But they won't do even that. Such a mega fraud doesn't concern them at all and they want everything around them spick and span, fair and correct! What does one call such a mentality, such an attitude, prevailing not only among members of this group but among the vast sea of human-beings? The infinite human stupidity?

Around hundred such senior bureaucrats (both in status and in age) are a big force, especially in the present age of social media. If just one of them alone could make and leave the mighty authorities and the mighty Supreme Court of India defenceless, just imagine what the tens of them could do if they wanted to do anything. It is true that everyone can't have the guts/confidence of the level required and couldn't take the extreme risk that had to be taken in taking on the all-powerful mafia and exposing it such that it has nothing to cover itself, standing naked in full public view!! Everyone can't know everything, in this case about an all-encompassing fraud merrily going on! But nothing of the

sort is required now. Everything is available on plate for the knowledge of and action by the rest of the world. People have only to pursue further in order to force the necessary all-round corrections - in the larger interest, in the interest of the coming generations, nothing in my personal interest at all. But none would do anything, they would only crib about this and that! And talk about everything else under the sun! Even the cream of the society – the members of this group!! Then what to talk of others, the lesser mortals? 😟😟

I felt aghast when a friend in another group, someone having retired at quite a senior public post, meant to convey quite recently that why should he or anyone else bother since it was my baby!! If someone tells the world about a big public crime happening, does it become his/her baby? The people, those at the receiving end of the crime (when a public crime takes place, all are at the receiving end directly or indirectly), don't have to bother at all? And this one is a crime unimaginably big, big beyond normal human comprehension, both in monetary, political, and other terms! Everything lies detailed in the public domain and in full knowledge of the Supreme Court of India, including the present CJI. I won't be surprised if many in this group, and most of the people outside this group, also felt same way as the above said friend of mine did. A sense of no concern and inaction by them all on such a massive continuing public crime (equivalent to thousands of murders) does indicate so. 😟

I may be wrong, but I feel that the retired people are better placed to act in the matter, since most of them no longer are at the mercy of the corporate or other authorities for their survival – at the mercy of those who are the perpetrators of the crime. Also otherwise, we are nearer to perishing, that is bound to happen sooner or later. Therefore, probably we have not much to lose,

but much more to gain for the coming generations, by forcing or by being instrumental for the necessary overdue corrections!

My apologies for any wrong utterances or anything that might have hurt!🙏 Thank you all!🙏"

The above post says a lot. I expected at least some brickbats from some group members. The group does consist of many members much senior to me in service and having retired at much higher rank than me (mostly they always keep quiet in the group). But thankfully, and to the credit of the group members, nothing of the sort happened. In fact, there hardly was any reaction of any kind. So, neither any positive came out of this post. But about a fortnight later, in response to another post by me (reproduced below),

'*Sadly what people are failing to understand is that the prosperity of the fraud despite being publicly exposed thoroughly and despite having been highlighted to possibly all the authorities and all those matter shows the meaninglessness of all the existing systems. In fact, it shows how we prefer to waste our lives in useless talks and things, not knowing or realising that we are doing so.* 😟😟', one of the admins of the group responded thus:

'Dear Atul ji,

Can you please spare this group from this issue? You have been raising this topic for last several years in this group and by now you might be clear about the interest or non-interest of the group members. I have been told by large number of group members from time to time that they are fed up with such posts. In case you still feel that any of the member is or will be of help to you on this issue to take up the cause further, you are requested to contact him directly on one to one basis.'

It appears to me that it was more the pent-up reaction to my earlier long post mentioned above. This response not only confirmed everything said in that post, but also confirms how even the best of the humans are governed by mob mentality, by their thoroughly conditioned minds, hardly capable of doing any original thinking or taking any worthwhile initiative in the larger interest. **They simply go the way the others go;** concerned about self-preservation first and foremost. They love to be shepherded, this way or that way. All the members of the group are otherwise very nice and kind people, probably much better beings than me. Probably, they are better men of the world. I have also been encouraged and helped on one-to-one basis in my endeavours/ in my journey, by some members of this very august group.

The above is not one-off example. I have highlighted it considering the stature of the members of this group. My efforts have met similar fate in other groups also. No one has ever felt/ shown much concern. They were, though, always seized of any issue raised in the media, howsoever petty or worthless – confirming their tendency to be just one of the mob.

There is another small group of my engineering batch-mates. They also are people who have retired from various high-ranking posts in various government or private organizations. The admin of this group and some members, to my utter shock, have expressed at times that the mega fraud in cricket was my personal issue/ baby and others need not be concerned with it (I gave a reference of this in the above long post also)!! Same way as one of the admins of the retired IRSS group mentioned in his retort to me, reproduced above. **I could never understand how a daily fraud in excess of 30 billion dollars a day was anybody's personal problem and didn't concern the rest of the world!!** Just because he/she was the first to expose it, it remained his/her personal baby for ever?

It doesn't pain me personally much anymore that there are people always ready with the brick-bats for me rather than appreciating my out of the world efforts in thoroughly exposing the mighty global mafia single handedly with such scientific evidence as none else could ever think of or ever attempted. There is not much appreciation for what all such efforts required, what risks had to be taken, what sacrifices had to be made! Because my earlier experiences in life have taught me to expect such behaviour from the mob that inhabits the mother earth in the form of the human-beings! **The mob has much greater appreciation for someone singing a song well.** 😀

I must be thankful to the group of the retired IRSS officers that I wasn't kicked out of the group even after the above big post. Seriously speaking, it has been their magnanimity. The cricket mafia and the Indian government probably have shown greater magnanimity in not liquidating/ harassing me till now. I am well aware of their limitless power. I do hope, for my own sake, that the magnanimity continues.😊

I am currently facing another expression of mob mentality. In my residential complex, maintenance of the building is being dealt with illegally and arbitrarily in many ways for many years. Yet, a large number of residents are for that to continue, believing in the power of the mob. The mob not only lynches, but even otherwise we are constantly a victim of the mob mentality; such is the human existence. A quote by George Carlin that *'Never underestimate the power of stupid people in a large group'* becomes very relevant.

Let us see the hard and harsh facts detachedly. We have seen how big a crime Cricket has been and how big a crime IPL-2023 was. Yet in long 10 years, not a single soul has felt any urge to take on this massive crime whole-heartedly, despite my best

efforts. Because there was no one to shepherd the mob to act against this crime! No one was shouting so from the TV channels; no newspaper headline ever screamed so. So, there is not much wonder that none of the authorities felt any inclination to do anything, as we have seen in an earlier chapter. The authorities, after all, are just a subset of the larger set that is society. Though, there is a difference. **The authorities were duty-bound to act, that is if duty had much meaning for them.**

❐

Manifestation of the Infinite Human Stupidity

When I was all at sea to understand the continued celebration or acceptance of a massive public crime by all those who never tired of making noise against petty wrongs around them or concerning them personally, who never tired of showing off their wisdom spurred on by their inherent ego every now and then; a quote by the great scientist Albert Einstein showed me some light. Einstein is known to have said, *"Two things are infinite: the universe and human stupidity; and I'm not sure about the universe."*

I find it very strange that the humanity never bothered to think or analyse why a genius of the calibre of Einstein made such a statement. Anyway, I could clearly see that a global sport having become a colossal crime and fraud, a fountainhead of corruption, and the vast sea of humanity continuing to celebrate it despite it lying publicly exposed so for a decade, the world remaining ignorant of the reality, was one of the manifestations of the infinite stupidity Einstein talked of. **Nothing else could explain it.**

The humans are a very egoist lot. So much so that the word 'stupidity' is an anathema to many. Their stupidity, in the form of ego, doesn't let them bother at all about the human stupidity, even when one of the known greatest living thinkers, Yuval Noah Harari, publicly expresses a big concern

for it. https://www.cnbc.com/2018/07/13/never-underestimate-human-stupidity-says-historian-and-author.html, and https://timesofindia.indiatimes.com/life-style/books/features/im-more-worried-about-the-dangers-of-natural-stupidity-than-ai-harari/articleshow/97835426.cms?from=mdr refer.

When something lies publicly exposed and proven as a monumental fraud and crime, and yet the media, both print and electronic, that controls the human endeavours and thoughts today, continues bombarding our consciousness round the clock parading it as a competitive sport; nothing but infiniteness of human stupidity alone can explain this phenomenon. The nonchalant acceptance of such existence by the humanity also can get explained by nothing else but infinite human stupidity.

A monumental fraud and crime are publicly taking place continuously and openly around you. And yet you don't feel any concern for it, but feel quite concerned at a news item of some scam worth a few lakhs of rupees or dollars (a negligible sum comparatively); what can you call it except infinite stupidity? When one fails to comprehend and appreciate the obvious, it has to be the infinite human stupidity behind it that Einstein talked of! It must be the infinite human stupidity behind the people spending their life times devoid of common-sense and sense of proportion; behind their getting ruled by mob mentality. Worried only about self-interest, they don't realise that their self-interest will get served much better if the larger interest was served!

The people who say that they need not bother about a monumental public fraud worth more than 30 billion dollars daily and its shameless continuous marketing as a competitive sport, and still feel themselves to be competent enough to give discourses on morality, right and wrong, and to give opinion

and judgement on everything under the sun; have to be in the clutches of nothing else but infinite human stupidity.

When the same executive and judiciary, the two powerful institutions evolved by humans, who dictate us and give us sermons on almost everything, themselves become the perpetrators and protectors of such an all-encompassing crime as Cricket or IPL, the infinite human stupidity gets manifested.

Humanity is known to have evolved over millions of years. It cherishes truth through religions followed or otherwise. And yet today it celebrates the biggest show of an exposed fraud. If that is not infinite stupidity (in this case underlined by infinite hypocrisy), what else that is? So much so, that through this collective pursuance of falsehood, all the wisdom evolved and being exchanged among the human beings dies a natural death. **On one hand, we continue to quote from various scriptures, we continue reminding others of great sayings by great saints, philosophers, seers, prophets, and leaders; and on the other hand, we act totally against those very scriptures and sayings by cherishing a monumental crime!** We get titillated by it!!

There are hundreds of millions of cricket bettors in the world. Even though most of them continue to lose heavily, they vastly remain ignorant of the reality of cricket, even though the same is in the public domain for a decade, even though books have been written with a purpose to help them. They continue to be in the clutches of the cricket and the betting mafia, continue to be exploited by them. What can explain it except infinite human stupidity?

There are tens of thousands of men and women of letters who share their wisdom on everything with the rest of the world. But most of them remain totally ignorant of how the world is

controlled by the mighty rogue forces. They don't know that cut off from the stark reality (the fact of control of the rogue forces becomes too evident when one contemplates over the continuing prosperity of the mega-frauds like cricket, and the thorough involvement of the vast media and the political leaders in it), whatever they say or think becomes meaningless, their whole existence not meaning much!!

This may sound as something very far-fetched to many, but unfortunately it can't be denied. **Once the humanity wakes up to the reality of a colossal fraud prospering for last 10 years even after having publicly been exposed repeatedly, everything is bound to become topsy-turvy, so extensive will the implications be.** For example, it will instantly occur to us that India-Pak enmity has been a big bogey for decades since the two countries have been playing fixed cricket matches between them, with full knowledge and blessings of their top political leaders. This, one necessary revelation itself is sufficient to agitate the consciousness of the citizens of these two countries in a big way. They will know the worthlessness of all the talk for decades associated with this bogey/fake enmity, and also of the wars/skirmishes between the two countries killing hundreds and thousands of braves on both the sides.

We shall know that all those, hundreds and thousands of them, whom we have been considering as super heroes and thorough gentlemen since our childhood, have been villains and criminals of the first order. We shall know how villainous the vast media has been, how it is totally controlled by some rogue forces! We shall know a lot about international politics and villainous side of many top leaders that we remain blissfully ignorant of. We shall know how unbelievably stupid we ourselves have been! **The human existence is bound to become topsy-turvy** (but for the better, I believe).

Also think of all the cricketers of past and present, all the officials, directly involved in this stupendous crime. What a false life and existence they have been living for material gains!!

I can go on and on, but I hope the readers would have understood how a thing they feel unconcerned about is a manifestation of the infinite stupidity that governs them, their king size ego notwithstanding.

Again, one may refer to my facebook post https://www.facebook.com/atulrailway/posts/pfbid0V1cEzE7MSRr6grhGgX3xKxcVtJEV8ZFxrvWsqLcUe3HauA73GPqf2qyqEPA6gModl dated 8th April, 2023. Probably it will help one understand the above better. It is reproduced below for ready reference:

"The Profound Stupidity

It was none other than Albert Einstein who said about a century ago, "Two things are infinite: the universe and human stupidity; and I'm not sure about the universe." It was a very pertinent statement from the great scientist, but I doubt if the humanity ever bothered, tried to overcome its inherent stupidity, or even ever tried to comprehend what Einstein said and why. Instead, it did continue to evolve with that very stupidity governing it all along. To be governed by mob mentality being just one such thing. Even the exposed rogues having maximum followers, in millions, on social networks, is nothing but an expression of that mob mentality and the inherent human stupidity. It was, therefore, not surprising, when probably the greatest thinker of modern times, Yuval Noah Harari, very recently came up with this: "I'm more worried about the dangers of natural stupidity than of artificial intelligence."

These two great persons must have had their own reasons to make above statements. Many others have experienced and said very pertinent things about human stupidity. But has all that been of any use? The human stupidity has ever been increasing! I give below here some very telling manifestations of the same in brief. Before that, going through this video also may be quite enlightening and helpful for the readers - https://www.youtube.com/watch?v=ww47bR86wSc .

Cricket is one of the most glaring manifestations of human stupidity. I pinpoint Cricket, and not any other sport here, because it is Cricket that is lying publicly exposed for about a decade now, well known to ICC also, what a monumental fraud it is! One may refer to the website thecricketmafia.com to know a lot more about it. The books listed therein detail almost everything. While such a stupendous fraud and crime continues unabated though it being publicly known for 10 very long years, being indulged in more and more by the perpetrators, ICC (International Cricket Council) being at the helm of it, what does the sea of humanity do? It doesn't ask any authority or anyone else any question about continuation of such an horrendous offence and crime, on the contrary it cheers the crime and the criminals!! The exposed and hence known criminals include among others the most cherished celebrities, the top industrialists, and the top leaders of the human world!! The Media still, most unashamedly, continues to bombard 24×7 the consciousness of the billions, through print and broadcast, with the nuances of Cricket, parading it as a competitive sport, and all the scripted and staged matches taking place round the clock and around the globe being paraded as a do or die battle! All that still could have been alright and would have not manifested human stupidity, but for the following!

The stark reality of cricket is in public domain for last decade, a very big time – equivalent to centuries of yonder - in the modern

world of advanced communication, yet it is to the credit of Media and human stupidity in general that even today the world largely remains unaware of the reality. That too, when I hardly left any stone unturned to make it known during first half of last decade by way of books, press conferences or knocking at all the possible authorities including Prime Minister of India, President of India, and the Supreme Court of India. For those who don't know, I shall very briefly narrate here again what the reality is and how its continuation shows the infinite human stupidity.

All or almost all the cricket matches taking place globally, league matches or international matches, women's cricket or men's cricket, are pre-scripted ball by ball and are nothing more than a staged drama. There already is an encyclopaedia of evidence in the public domain to show and prove it. And when daily newspapers and round the clock TV channels still (ten years after the fact was made known to the Media) continue to hide the fact from the public, and report on these otherwise, the world at large continuing to lap all that up as something official and authentic; the human stupidity does touch infinite proportions.

As I am editing this write-up, I give a very recent example for those to readily understand everything, who really want to understand and are not stupid beyond redemption. In the KKR vs GT match on the 9th April, 2023, in IPL-16, a batsman of KKR continuously hit 5 sixes of the last 5 balls to notch up the required 28 runs and win the match. Everyone was brain-washed by the commentators and other experts crowding the world that it was a great batting that won the match for KKR. Did it occur to cricket viewers or did anyone tell us through print or on air that the consecutive five sixes were necessarily facilitated by the bowler by bowling such balls that could conveniently be hit for six after six? This is just one crude example, a very recent one, being given here for one to be able to understand and grasp

what is what by slight application of mind to the above; without having to go through the existing encyclopaedia of evidence.

When the same vast sea of humans, especially the tens of millions of highly educated and learned, refuse to bother a bit about this stupendous crime equivalent to open murders and loot (again it is a matter of record that the loot is worth tens of billions of dollars daily by the betting syndicates) with the involvement of almost all those who are running the world, but continue to crib and complain about all other sorts of wrong doings, comparatively very petty, many of those even not proved, what Einstein said or meant starts becoming clear. Mainly two things, absence of common-sense and the absence of sense of proportion among humans, underline the infinite human stupidity Einstein talked of. No one, public or the authorities, the leaders or the Media, is even remotely bothered about a proven continuous open public loot worth billions of dollars a day, but they all do raise the roof even for suspected loots worth pennies (at least comparatively) here and there. And again, they all include the most learned and educated amongst us, tens of millions of those. I doubt if any word other than 'infinite' could be used for such stupidity!

It is nothing less than a miracle that having to survive in the same world, I have been able to continuously expose and prove the stupendous continuous crime by the mightiest in the world. Strange are the ways of God! I am well aware that there is no dearth of die-hard conditioned and blocked minds who feel that I am unduly obsessed with cricket. I feel amazed that they don't realize that now it is no more fraudulent cricket and the phenomenal loot through it that matters so much, but what matters much more now is the continuance of the enormous crime and fraud internationally, despite lying so thoroughly and so repeatedly exposed, and the overall infinite human stupidity that gets depicted by this very fact. And please rest assured;

this stupidity is not only self-defeating and self-damaging, but also self-killing for the humanity!! We see its self-killing effect periodically during wars, and saw it in full flow very recently during Covid times.

Humans have evolved creating Judiciary and treating it as Supreme. When the same judiciary lies thoroughly exposed for failing in its duties, openly lets a stupendous crime and fraud continue despite having been made aware of it and having been urged to control it, thus itself becoming a stigma on humanity (the book 'We the Oodles' refers), neither the vast judicial or legal world of India nor the rest of the world bothers or acts/ reacts a bee wit, and the humanity continues as ever with the totally failed judiciary or judicial systems largely controlling its existence, considering the same still as Supreme as ever – the human stupidity. glares us in the face. There is no introspection of any kind anywhere!! That is another very clear manifestation of the infinite human stupidity that Einstein indicated.

Probably nothing underlined the infinite human stupidity more than the recent genocide through Covid and vaccines, and the actions/reactions of the humans throughout the ordeal and after that. As was bound to happen, many righteous men and women from all around the globe have come out with hard facts and scientific logic to expose that Genocide. But as with the fraudulent cricket, the world continues to hail and cheer the very perpetrators of the Genocide. The rogue Media remained at the helm of this Genocide as well. The book 'What is killing us... Covid or Stupidity?' may refer here.

Not only tens of millions across the world perished, the nears and dears of those who survived; most of those surviving are also left with highly compromised health, and a much-heightened sense about uncertainty of life. And still, instead

of bothering as to how and why such a Genocide took place leaving the survivors with a much worse quality of life, or bothering to prosecute the mass murderers, some of them well known; those surviving are again busy only in talking shop. If that is not infinite stupidity, then what is? The inherent stupidity has also prevented man to take note of and ponder over the fact how religion had become totally insignificant those days!! I say this with due respect to all the religions. Covid per se, even forgetting that it was a Genocide, necessitated man to do a lot of introspection, and change/mend his ways. Nothing of the sort ever happened. We all know how the world continues in same merry way, or even worse!!

While the human world continues to be in the total grip of an open elephantine crime and fraud, publicly exposed for long 10 years, and smarting from a very recent Genocide, what do the tens or hundreds of millions of the intellectuals inhabiting the earth do? Unmindful of and oblivious of these harsh realities, choosing to be blind to these, they continue with indulging in worthless talks, parading their religious, spiritual, and all other sorts of wisdom, mostly hollow and inconsequential, worrying a lot about history, feeling proud of technical and scientific progresses etc. The inherent infinite stupidity of humans doesn't let these men and women, all the great preachers and leaders and their followers also included, realize that everything else has been meaningless when they have been accepting to be in the clutches of such a fraudulent and murderous world with full knowledge for many years now!!

Yes, one has to fight for daily survival alright, but that doesn't necessitate that one must remain profoundly stupid. I don't know whether they realize it or not, in the bargain the people around me have chosen to die even more stupid than they were born! Good or bad, they are going to leave a more stupid world for the

coming generations. The infinitely stupid humans have evolved with something called Media and now they have become a toy in the hands of that very Media that has turned totally rogue!! This all is chronicled in details for those who would like to know.

The above are only a few manifestations and indications of the infinite stupidity Einstein talked of.

The question that arises is whether we humans should accept our stupidity as unconquerable, or should come together to overcome it for our own good and betterment!!"

Let us see this very recent news item (I came across this when the drafting of this book was in the final phase) https://economictimes.indiatimes.com/news/sports/anti-corruption-activists-demand-match-fixing-probe-against-sri-lanka-over-defeat-to-india/articleshow/103761332.cms?from=mdr. It states:

'Cricket fans and anti-corruption activists have demanded for a police probe on malpractices and alleged match fixing over Sri Lanka's humiliating defeat against India at the Asia Cup final on Sunday.

A civil rights organisation, Citizen Power Against Bribery, Corruption and Wastage filed a complaint at the Police Headquarters in Colombo alleging that there is a serious suspicion over Sri Lankan cricketers' performance and specially getting out for such a small number of runs.

The chairman of the organisation, C. Kamantha Thushara, complained that there is a serious suspicion over match fixing as Sri Lanka was all out for 50 runs within just 15.2 overs.'

This news is related to the Asia Cup final between India and Sri Lanka played on the 17th September, 2023 at Colombo.

Such a complaint is being made 10 years after the world has been shown how cricket was scripted and fixed ball-by-ball. One, people are unaware of the reality even after 10 long years because they are in the clutches of a criminal media. Two, it does indicate infinite human stupidity if the world continues to be as ignorant as the above news item clearly indicates. **Someone is suspecting some match to be fixed even now, while the reality of total match-fixing in Cricket already lies established beyond doubt, in the same human world in which he lives, 10 long years ago, having been reinforced many times since then.**

Does above not indicate total inadequacy of our evolved systems, inter-alia manifesting infinite human stupidity?

It is another matter that many such and much more serious news items have appeared and disappeared over past many years, no logical conclusion of any being known. In the meantime, the crime through fraudulent Cricket has not only been continuing unbridled, but has been prospering by leaps and bounds; confirming the existence of the infinite human stupidity 😟.

One may come across many more manifestations of human stupidity. Probably, wars are the biggest such manifestation. The infinite human stupidity is not something that can just be wished away. Unfortunately, **'Law of Collective Stupidity'** (propounded in the book '*What is killing us... Covid or Stupidity?*') does hold.

Today, hardly anyone comprehends or appreciates the import of human stupidity. Even if slightly aware, people tend to close their minds to it. That doesn't make it any less significant. The fact that even Mr Harari feels most worried about natural stupidity, even more than the artificial intelligence, should make all of us worry. Then, we shall do something to fix a thing we feel worried about.😊

❒

Revisiting Covid Times

It is worthwhile revisiting Covid times of 2020 and 2021, to understand the infinite human stupidity even better. Many revelations came out then and many more have come out since then through very authentic books or otherwise from many renowned people telling the world how Covid and vaccines were a very big fraud wreaked on the vast humanity globally. Many actions, some by governments, now and then, have further been confirming it. Millions-nears and dears of tens of millions of us- lost their lives. And tens of millions of us are surviving with compromised health thereafter.

Yet hardly anyone of us is bothered. The rogue forces that combined to bring on that misery on the humanity are absolutely free to strike anytime again. Not only that, we, the victims, have been hailing many responsible for that genocide (loosely so called) as our top beloved leaders.

One Dr Vernon Coleman has written more than one detailed book telling us all about the genocidal fraud. And yet some are too happy to just dismiss him as a *conspiracy theorist*. This is how the human stupidity works.

This makes stupidity a very worrisome commodity. Please appreciate it is our collective stupidity that I talk of. **Millions of lives were recently lost, and we, the surviving ones also can lose our lives, something too precious to us, any time, because of our infinite stupidity.**

That is because we have not been questioning the rogue forces as we must have been doing. The rogue forces as detailed in some previous chapters, have been the same; whether behind Covid or behind the Mount Everest of crime and corruption.

❐

Myself and the World

I intend to bring out only as much in this chapter as I feel necessary in the context of this book.

I start with my facebook post https://www.facebook.com/atulrailway/posts/pfbid05ipd1Sq5ik778j1W4Pg4ges3f96CbQdRLJ5CE8qoviF2nsn6drg8wxaqHUHE4dn5l of the 15th October, 2022. Here I reproduce it for ready reference.

'The pain of being Atul Kumar

This heading may appear to be narcissistic to many at a first casual glance. But I am sure they would soon realize what it is all about as they assimilate the following brief.

It was about 10 long years ago that, for the first time, it was revealed to the world by me that an international sport as vast and as popular as Cricket was a charade, a thoroughly fixed and scripted joke controlled from outside the playing fields. People passionately follow Cricket like a religion in most of the countries it is played in, especially in the populous Asian countries. They consider it a clean and above-board game of gentlemen. Just imagine the blasphemy of such an abuse of their faith in the sport, and also the import of my efforts.

In doing what I did, I stuck my neck out, and risked the wrath of the all-powerful betting mafia and the collective might of thousands of celebrities from Cricket and other walks

of life. I knew I was inviting the ridicule of millions of common people and intellectuals who were and are just incapable of comprehending the stark reality (it is their limitation as God made them, nothing else). I was all alone – very, very alone, standing against them all, all these long years.

The people who never took the trouble to understand what was the basis of my assertions that appeared impossible to be true, led by nothing but their conditioned beliefs, ridiculed me left and right. Many of them were people very close to me - my relations and friends. That was very painful for me on the personal front. I hope some of them might have realized by now how wrong they were, but not one of them has accepted it and said sorry to me. Most of them still feel happy in their blessed ignorance. That is how people, especially intellectuals, are governed by nothing but ego. Probably my biggest personal pain has been and is that those closest to me, my very own, my nears and dears, personify the petty ego, self-contradictions, the hypocrisy and the resultant stupidity the most!! But this write-up is not to complain about such pains. I know that many mortals have had to suffer much greater pain personally.

This is to tell how painful it is to see the humanity all around me totally drenched in rank hypocrisy and stark stupidity. My books, especially the book 'What is killing us... Covid or Stupidity?', bring this out with vivid details. I doubt if even the millions who lost their very own during those two years or so due to unfathomable collective stupidity ever bothered to make themselves aware of what was behind that genocide. Many more, still suffering the aftermath of the planned genocide themselves, also are not bothered. All this doesn't harm me personally or alone; it harms the sea of humanity itself.

To helplessly see that happening and my sustained efforts of 10 years failing to make any dent is too painful, a deep pain I have to live with till my breaths continue. Millions died in the world since my efforts had failed (it is explained in the above book). That pain is peculiar to Atul Kumar because anyone can see (if one tries) how these unprecedented and unparalleled efforts in human history had and have miserably failed. The rank hypocrisy and the stark stupidity still continue to rule the roost. The continuing parading of cricket matches round the clock and around the globe as something competitive (despite enormous international implications of such a public fraud), even 10 long years after the truth became public, shows it too well.

Before exposing Cricket, while working in the Indian Railways, I had also exposed how approximately Rs. 5000 crores of public money was getting leaked annually due to procurement through cartels. Despite a formed committee (I was part of it) suggesting solutions to overcome that leakage to a large extent, the systems leading to the leakage have continued unhindered.

My greatest disappointment came from the much-hyped Supreme Court of India. My book 'We the Oodles', published about two years ago, details its indefensible and unpardonable sins. And yet, the sea of intelligentsia continues to hail the same Supreme Court of India, choosing to remain unmindful of the reality.

The very serious indefensible criminality of thousands of celebrities and powerful people from many walks of life, including politics and the corporate world, lies repeatedly exposed publicly for last many years. Yet, the world that

makes a lot of noise about isolated crimes and some suspected criminals has been dead quiet for years about these thousands of times bigger crimes and the thousands of proven criminals. I feel aghast when I see the same very intellectuals, around me and otherwise, mired in hypocrisy and stupidity, showcasing their knowledge and wisdom on every issue under the sun.

There is no dearth of people in the world who take pride in their religion and scriptures. Yet, when the religions and scriptures of the world lie so blatantly abused by public celebration of a monumental fraud by those very people, the pain multiplies!!

I am destined to die unknown and unsung when my time comes. That hardly matters. But what matters is that, in contrast, the proven criminals, myriad of them, are today the super-heroes for the masses. Great public honours also have been bestowed on some of them. The falsity continues to be reinforced by none other than the media and the showbiz industry.

To understand all this as well as hardly anybody else comprehends, to suffer it, and yet having to survive in the same world is the pain of being Atul Kumar. The pain of being Atul Kumar is the pain of a common man who had firm convictions in common sense, straightforwardness, and the larger good, in contrast to a world around him driven by unflinching mob mentality and self-interest.'

Reflecting on the above today, I doubt if even the above seemingly strong words sufficed to bring out my pain that resulted from the deep sense of hopelessness and helplessness, I had been living with for last some years. Probably my helplessness has been as infinite as the human stupidity or idiocy. And probably no words can express something infinite!

It has been really tough to know how stupid the humanity was and yet to live within the framework of the same world. **Saying this in no way means to demean many great human virtues such as love and compassion. Neither it is to demean the inherent goodness of most of the individuals.** But imagine, how much better the life would have been for the vast sea of humanity, if the egoist man ever thought of shedding/ overcoming hypocrisy and stupidity; rather than indulging in immaterial issues, idle talks, and in exchanges of half-cooked wisdom, throughout life.

Understanding and knowing how improbable or impossible it was for our deeply and thoroughly conditioned minds even to comprehend the reality of Cricket and the world, I thought of, worked on, and was lucky enough to come out with the scientific evidence (so that no ifs and buts could have any place) 10 years ago, detailed in my book 'Bettors Beware.' 10 years is a long time and ICC (International Cricket Council) is a very powerful organization. Yet, none in this big world, full of scholars and highly learned people, ever countered that mathematical/ scientific evidence. **On the contrary, on record is the confirmation of it by two men of some repute, very well versed with the world of sports, an Indian and an Englishman.** Today that evidence lies so thoroughly vindicated even otherwise that it is good that no one even attempted to counter it ever. To my mind, that was a very extra-ordinary achievement for the human world. **Applying those principles as detailed in the book, fixing in any cricket match gets easily proved, just from the score books. And waking up to the reality of Cricket and all that it implies at any point of time is bound to revolutionize the whole human world!** So vast and deep are the implications!!

The scientific evidence, and the encyclopaedia of other evidence since then, are such that anyone trying to dismiss me as a conspiracy theorist (a commonly easy tool in the hands of the pseudo intellectuals) will himself look like a very big fool.

It is extreme bad luck of us all that we have already wasted 10 long years.

Let us see who I am and what my credentials were before I single-handed took on the rest of the world on the subject of Cricket, and won hands down. I am a normal man of the world, sufficiently educated, with some academic achievements as well. I successfully competed through All India Engineering Services exam of 1979, conducted by Union Public Service Commission (UPSC) in India, to join Indian Railways Stores Service (IRSS). I was born in a lower middle-class family (financially/economically) but to great parents (I reckon so). It is for the people to judge whether I have been logical or a lunatic! 😊

If I were not a lunatic, which I hope I am not😊, then was it not necessary for the world to react to the sensational exposures by me a decade ago on Cricket through my published interviews and press conferences etc.? Was it not necessary for it to prove me wrong and if so, to deal with me strongly under the laws for spreading canards irresponsibly? Or to take suitable actions if I was right? How could a world full of millions of educated and intelligent men and women simply keep quiet and let such a massive open public fraud continue and prosper?

I can understand that the people are keen to continue with their entertainment through sports, having been addicted to that, even if it is all false. But what about the tens of millions of their brethren becoming broke because of the

falsehood, because of the fraud? What about the very vast and deep other implications they have been unaware of? There was a way out that came to my mind years ago and was suggested through one of my press releases. We continue to market cigarettes along with a statutory warning 'smoking is injurious to health.' Similarly, we could continue with all our cricket matches and their broadcast to keep entertaining the public, with a statutory warning, **'this match could be fixed.'** 😁😁. Of course, this would have cooked the goose of the mafia and a very big fraud industry.😊

In service, I mostly found myself on the wrong side of my bosses. IRSS must be a decades old cadre, hundreds of highly qualified and competent men and women having been its luminaries. And yet, it was only I who was instrumental in publicly bringing out that there was estimated leakage to the tune of Rs 5000 crores annually to the public exchequer on account of procurement from cartels. That was after my repeated in-house efforts for any effective action failed. The peculiarity was that the organization itself created the cartels, subsequently to be fleeced by those. It was first big case of systemic corruption, that got exposed as a result of my efforts. I was quite aware of the implied threats to my well-being in many ways, in doing what I did then. But that didn't deter me. For the simple reason that at that time I valued Rs 5000 crores per annum of public money much higher than an individual's (that is my own) wellbeing. Fortunately or unfortunately, **I have always had that sense of proportion.**

The purpose of above is not to boast, as most of the minds would tend to think, but to look at myself or rather my efforts objectively.

If someone from IRSS or Railways were to tell you that it is all bunkum, please don't believe him. One, even the Railways never countered it. Two, it was later on confirmed through a report by none other than the Metro Man, Mr E. Sreedharan. And there is more to it.

The usual happened at last in this case. The Railways formed a committee to suggest the systemic corrections to the existing procedures that had been leading to the formation of cartels. I was also given the opportunity to work in that committee. Against all the odds, I was successful in ensuring that the report of the committee was submitted, before I took voluntary retirement in end, 2011. Alas! Again, as usual, nothing good happened. The bureaucratic inaction prevailed and the procurement through cartels has been continuing. **So much so that another officer of IRSS has been fighting hard to control the menace of cartels among other things in one Railway unit as I am drafting this.**

As mentioned above, what I could do in the Railways was unprecedented, and in all probability will remain the only effort of this kind ever. My ordeals those years are a matter of record. Those became fresh in my memory when I was browsing through the related papers recently.

Then I was fighting a very big and mighty organization from within for the right cause. For last ten years my fight has been against a thousands times bigger and more powerful mafia controlling the world, while I continue to live/survive in the very same world! **I was all alone then and I am all alone now**, though having got moral and other support at times from a few on both the occasions; **even though the cause for my fight has been to benefit the vast humanity each time.**

It does please me that no one has ever been able to counter me logically, with regards to my unprecedented and sensational exposes related to the procurement from cartels in the Indian Railways or related to Cricket. Again, that has its objective worth also.

While it might have pleased me, but it has served a very big purpose for the mafia and the rogue forces. Any attempt by anyone to counter me would have resulted in more and more people knowing about the reality, without any chance of succeeding for him/her. The rogue forces knew it was impossible for them to prove my contention wrong. **They know the truth alright.** It is for this reason that there was no counter to my petition even in the Supreme Court by any authority. To keep quiet and let the matter lie buried suited their very purpose of continuing with the mega-fraud. **They just couldn't let the people at large know of the reality of Cricket. With the media and all the authorities including judiciary being on their side (proof of the pudding is in the eating),** to keep everything buried, away from the public eye, was not and has not been much difficult for the mafia.

The media and the authorities of the world now know or are supposed to know for last 10 years the reality of Cricket, as a result of my efforts (even though I never belonged to the world of Cricket 😊). Today that reality is too open. And yet any newspaper or sports or news channel most shamelessly bombards us 24×7 with the narration of competitive cricket. Probably it is that arrogant falsity, the open criminality, that has kept me spurred on all these years. That has been besides my sense of proportion**, since I find the fraud to be too big to be ignored and forgotten.**

All the people around me have ego. **I do wonder what happens to their ego when they accept being fooled so openly and continuously?** Why don't they act and react? How can the same people who talk so big about anything else, who enter into big debates on historical events and developments, or any other matter, the accomplished professionals, the preachers, **the legal luminaries** et al accept so nonchalantly being fooled round the clock (through continuous marketing of a mega-fraud as some competitive sport)? What becomes of their ego and social existence?

With this, another very interesting question comes up. Humans have instinctive curiosity. They enjoy suspense fiction as it raises their curiosity and then satiates it. The real-life murders and other crimes interest many. In the form of Cricket, a massive and mind-boggling fraud is openly taking place 24×7 before their very eyes. There must be some modus-operandi to it, which remains too puzzling. And yet no one appears to be curious to know about it!!

The advantage I have been having is that I now know the hollowness and worthlessness of the human world, of the big opinion pieces in newspapers, of the TV debates, of the speeches by political leaders etc., since the existing world is subservient to a very big mafia; most of the intellectuals being either unaware of or incapable of comprehending the reality. I don't waste my time and energy on worthless issues anymore. Also, I do feel extremely fulfilled for all what I could do, despite my many shortcomings.😊

Probably, the toughest part of my journey with regards to the mega-fraud has been to continue to have unflinching faith in common-sense and self. Ten years ago, I went public against

the belief, hardened over a few decades, of the rest of the world. Initially for many years, many of those around me made fun of me, the reality being incomprehensible for them. On the face of it, it is still unbelievable. But, today, everything not only lies vindicated, but is also open (thru hundreds of tipsters crowding the social media), except for the die-hard blinds and/or fools.

Do I get hailed by the world for my efforts? The answer is a very big No. I did get national level award, S R Jindal Prize 2011 for crusade against corruption, for my efforts related to Railways that time, but since then I have seen that hardly anyone around me considers it as any worthwhile achievement. Though, the press probably did value my credibility because of it when I initially exposed the reality of Cricket.

The post from one of the admins of the Whatsapp group of retired IRSS officers reproduced in an earlier chapter typifies how the world values me and treats me. **It considers me as a villain, trying to disturb its peace!** All humans have their own limitations and vision (channelled?) to value anything. But it is the very same world for whose overall betterment I have been toiling with all my God given attributes! I could expose and publicly prove a global crime involving a fraud estimated to be worth in excess of 30 billion dollars a day. That is only Cricket; I have shown earlier how there have to be similar frauds going on in other sports, some of those much bigger than Cricket. The money that gets looted belonged to hundreds of millions of innocent cricket and other sports bettors world-wide. Earlier I had tried to save annual leakage of public money worth Rs 5000 crores. Have both of these been matters of personal concern for me?

The retort referred in the above para (l repeat, it is not one-off reaction, but the general feeling of those around me) does

send the message to me and the world, "**whether humans are infinitely stupid or not, only stupid will think of the larger good and really bother for the welfare of the mankind. The wise will only pretend**."😁 It is a matter of record that many common people who sacrificed their lives for the right causes are a forgotten lot today, while the criminals and the rogues have large followings.

It is true that when I understood and exposed the crime and corruption in cricket more than 10 years ago, I found that my own efforts earlier related to Indian Railways, though unprecedented, paled in comparison; and hence governed by my sense of proportion I didn't spend any more time and energy on that subject (probably I had already done my utmost in that issue, probably not).

The world was required to react to and act on my exposure 10 years ago. It did nothing. **As a result, my 10 precious years have been wasted in repeating the same things again and again while trying to wake the world up.** Many will say, **and honestly many, even in my family,** say or feel that I have been foolish in persisting when the world was not interested (just like the retort from the admin of the Whatsapp group). I am sure many close to me must be feeling sick of me. Do I forget everything, the continuing fraud, the real concern for wellbeing of the world at a very large scale, just because the others feel that I should? Should my thought process be limited by the other minds?

The compassionate world must realize what would be my psyche over last 10 years; the psyche of a man who took utmost risk and succeeded in exposing a monumental public fraud, succeeded in proving it beyond any ifs and buts,

continued to pursue the very big cause at his own cost (other costs being much greater than the monetary costs) leaving no stone unturned, and yet there are no serious takers of the cause till date. Not only that, the fraud continues to prosper by leaps and bounds!! How should I be feeling? **People may try to put themselves in my shoes!**

The humanity could have utilised me (having some special God given attributes, as it appears now🤔) and my time for some more productive use, by having acted on the exposure of the massive public fraud 10 years ago. But alas! Everyone appears to be busy in self-service and self-preservation, not prepared to think for the greater causes. The people expect similar behaviour from others, especially if they are family or friends.😟

My simple questions are: **By what scripture, by what law, supported by which preaching or saying, for what larger good, or why else does a monumental crime continue prospering even after lying publicly exposed and proved not for a few days, weeks, or months, but for more than 10 years? Which religion permits it? Why are those who give sermons on religion, morality, and many other issues, those who express their knowledge and wisdom on thousands of matters, on everything under the sun, silent on this Mount Everest of crime and corruption? Why are the political and corporate leaders et al silent? Which good morning message, out of the thousands being circulated/exchanged on the social media, justifies or supports the monumental fraud? Why and how has the world been accepting the corrupt sports as a way of life, given all the accumulated wisdom it never tires boasting of? How can anyone, any celebrity or any leader or anyone else, be great or of value**

in a world that celebrates total falsehood? Probably, in such questions lies the essence of this book.

When I listen to Amitabh Bachhan emotionally reciting poems like *'agnipath agnipath agnipath……'*, or political leaders or Ministers making valuable sounding speeches or statements, or renowned preachers explaining philosophical nitty-gritties and giving apparently very meaningful advices, or when I read so much wisdom contained in various books, etc., I do wonder. I wonder, what happens to all these seemingly great and wise people that they gleefully accept a world that continues to celebrate an exposed and open massive to the power of massive fraud!! Is it their ignorance (that should be a matter of big concern for the humanity if those considered great remain so hopelessly ignorant even a decade after everything becoming public), concern only for self, extreme hypocrisy, or the infinite human stupidity at work?

Similarly, I wonder when I see the common intellectuals, active or very active on the social media, talk and worry about everything under the sun, but choosing to tightly shut their eyes when it comes to the highly visible Mount Everest of Crime and Corruption.

Let us once again try to understand and appreciate the amounts involved in ongoing frauds through sports betting. The amounts involved in Cricket alone should be sufficient to sustain the world population. If we add the amounts involved in soccer and other sports, more than one such worlds can be sustained. The people around me are worried and bothered about negligible frauds/scams in comparison involving this or that person. **But such a big continuous fraud involving the mightiest of the world doesn't concern them!!** On the contrary, as mentioned earlier, they consider me as a villain

of some kind who bothers them for something that is useless or is his personal issue/baby and doesn't or shouldn't concern them at all. Those indulged in and responsible for such big frauds resulting in miseries to the masses are the super heroes for them and the ignorant victims. **The masses for whose very welfare I have been toiling are not even remotely aware of my existence.** There is no recognition of any kind for my efforts that have been unprecedented and probably will remain unparalleled in the human history.

Let us reflect here for a moment who the masses are and what their compulsions are? The masses are people like you and me. Like me, they have to survive in this very world as it is. They have to work and they have to make compromises. They have to look after their health and of those in the family. They have to look after family. Many have to fight battle for daily survival. The masses bother a lot about material gains. In short, they are busy in mundane activities and existence. Mostly they always are in awe of the government and the authorities, whether they are on the right or wrong side of law. Their instinct for self-preservation doesn't let them take on the authorities, at least not in matters not concerning them directly. They fail to realise and appreciate that the larger good and halting a very big public loot will ultimately benefit them all in big way, whatever be their status. They always give their immediate self-interest a big priority. **They shun Truth if they perceive it to be coming in the way of their immediate interests.** They get ruled by hypocrisy, ego, and the mob mentality (natural attributes of human beings).

There is a very big number of very well-off and well-fed people also. They feel too happy with their own fate to bother about any larger good. They just rake in money and enjoy life.

Almost all of us have our own sins to worry about and be afraid of; that deters us to raise voice against the continuing massive public frauds, and the powerful mafia controlling the governments, howsoever we ourselves be affected by such frauds. And many, of course, lack the necessary intelligence and vision to grasp.

The above applies to all, whether great activists or otherwise. Everyone likes and tends to remain in one's own comfort zone; whatever be one's financial or other status. That's the crux. Talking about sundry things including corruption is mostly only time-pass for all. If that were not so, how is it that there is not even a single another person today in this big world questioning the Mount Everest of crime and corruption whole heartedly? How is it that this Mount Everest of public crime and corruption continues to gain height daily?

Whatever it is, it can't be people's fault. Unknowingly, they have been conditioned so thoroughly since childhood about many things, that they fail to comprehend what they must for their own welfare (mine also must be a conditioned mind 😊). **They are victims of the human world as it has evolved.**

Still, all the people must think: if a loot of the order of tens of billions of dollars (should be in excess of a hundred of billions of dollars, if we think of all the sports, especially football) is taking place daily, where that money comes from and how they all are bound to gain a lot if that loot (**and all the falsity that leads to that loot**) stops or gets curbed. Those enormous amounts now going to a few pockets will come back to the public system, will be available for utilisation by the masses.

The greatest concern for the masses is to make both ends meet. Some even indulge in crime just for that. Please do think; will not the daily survival become much easier for the masses, with the amounts being looted through IPL, Cricket, and other sports available in the main stream?

The people must also think how worthwhile it is for them to spend whole life complaining and bothering about comparatively petty wrong-doings in hundreds of spheres through tens of expressions; while continuing to accept the cache and reserve of much magnified wrong-doings i.e., IPL and Cricket, nonchalantly.

In the end, I must say that all said and done, it is the world as it exists that has been sustaining me, and it is in this very world that my past writings have come out with the help of many people, as hopefully this book also will. Whatever I have done or achieved, has been in this very world as it exists.

❏❏❏

About the Author

Atul Kumar is an engineer, a postgraduate from IIT Madras. He served the Indian Railways as a Class I officer from 1981 to 2011 before taking voluntary retirement. While in service, he was instrumental in exposing leakage of approximately Rs 5000 crores per year through cartels in Railway procurement. As a consequence, he was awarded S R Jindal Prize 2011 for crusade against corruption at the national level.

Atul Kumar is also an awarded poet in Hindi. Many of his poetry books have been published.

About a decade ago, after retirement, Atul Kumar exposed the ball-by-ball institutionalised fixing in Cricket through his books and press conferences etc.

Atul Kumar also wrote a book on the genocide through Covid in English. The same has been published in Hindi also. Since then, his conclusions on this subject also are being continuously validated through various exposures on the subject, nationally and internationally.

Most of the books written by him can be seen through this link: https://www.amazon.in/kindle-dbs/entity/author/B0BKFSBLDV?_encoding=UTF8&node=976389031&offset=0&pageSize=12&searchAlias=stripbooks&sort=author-sidecar-rank&page=1&langFilter=default#formatSelectorHeader.

Many of these books, including the poetry ones, have no parallel.

Email: atulrailway@hotmail.com